# THE FACE OF WALES

# BOOKS ON WALES

## THE LAND OF WALES

### By Eiluned and Peter Lewis

Containing 128 pages of text, nearly 140 illustrations from photographs and a colour frontispiece.

*Demy 8vo.* *Third edition*

" *A majestic chronicle —with a selection of the best photographs that have ever been included in a publication dealing with Wales.*"—The Western Mail.

" *Read this bright, attractive book and study its beautiful illustrations.*"—The Sunday Times.

## WELSH BORDER COUNTRY

### By P. Thoresby Jones

With a colour frontispiece, more than 120 photographic illustrations and 128 pages of comprehensive text.

*Demy 8vo.* *Third edition*

" *The book is a very good book, well produced and beautifully illustrated. The author's style is admirable.*"—The Field.

" *One murmurs 'Exquisite', sadly wishing that that much overworked word could be reserved for such worthy occasions as this.*"—The Observer.

## WELSH COUNTRY UPBRINGING

### By D. Parry-Jones

Containing 144 pages of text, a colour frontispiece and nearly 90 photographic illustrations.

*Demy 8vo.* *Second edition*

" *It is a privilege to go back in company with Mr. Parry-Jones fifty years in Carmarthenshire and enter a world that used to be the normal one but has now passed away. . . . The illustrations are so good that they hurt !* "

—J. S. Collis in *Time and Tide.*

## BATSFORD BOOKS

MONTGOMERY

Lymore

Llanwynog

Plynlimon

*1*

Nanteos

*2*

Cascob

Radnor Forest

NEW

Ystrad Flur Abbey

Knill

RADNOR

*3*

R. Irfon

Capel y ffin

R. Wye

*4*

Bronllys Castle

ansawel

Llandovery

BRECON

R. Towy

Llangorse Lake

Black Mts

Llanthony

nevor astle

Penpont

Llanspyddyd

Tretower

Patrishow

Llandilo

Crickhowell

olden Grove

Castle Coch

R. Neath

R. Usk

MERTHYR TYDFIL

*7*

R. Taff

SWANSEA

Neath

R. Rhondda

Caerphilly

E R

NEWPORT

Parkmill

Margam

Coity Castle

Ruperra Cas.

Cefn Mably

St. Fagan's Castle

CARDIFF

Ewenny Priory

LLANDAFF

Beaupre Castle

St. Donats Castle

Llantwit

10    20    30    Miles

1   The Brecon Beacons

*Reproduced from the
painting by Norman Janes*

# THE
# FACE OF WALES

*By*

TUDOR EDWARDS

B. T. BATSFORD LTD.

LONDON    NEW YORK

TORONTO    SYDNEY

To
My Mother
DILYS EDWARDS
And
The Memory of My Father
CHARLES HYWEL EDWARDS

*First published, Spring* 1950

PRINTED AND BOUND IN GREAT BRITAIN BY
WILLIAM CLOWES AND SONS, LTD., LONDON AND
BECCLES, FOR THE PUBLISHERS, B. T. BATSFORD,
LTD. LONDON : 15 NORTH AUDLEY STREET, W.1
AND MALVERN WELLS, WORCESTERSHIRE.
NEW YORK : 122 EAST 55TH STREET.
TORONTO : 103 ST. CLAIR AVENUE WEST.
SYDNEY : 156 CASTLEREAGH STREET

# PREFACE

THE problem presented in writing yet another book on Wales is somewhat akin to the compiling of an anthology : it is not so much a question of what to put in as what to leave out. Obvious difficulties arise in a survey of a large area which is heterogeneous alike as to physical features and the life of the people within the area. My policy therefore has been to dwell upon those aspects largely neglected by topographers rather than on the more familiar ground.

That there are such aspects there is no doubt. Post-Reformation architecture, for example, remains almost untouched, for it has been deplorably neglected by all travellers in Wales. Even George Borrow was sadly deficient in those things which we particularly seek, whether it be architecture, costume or Caerphilly cheese. To each his own shibboleths.

This book has been mainly designed for the Sassenach who thinks of Wales only in terms of the Rhondda Valley, the playgrounds of the northern littoral, *et id genus omne*, as well as for those Anglo-Welsh condemned to live away from their Hesperides. But I hope, and believe, that Welsh people too will find something new and will be stimulated to further searching in their own land.

One apology must be made. I have drawn an arbitrary line from north to south which excludes Monmouthshire, but although this conforms to the latest report issued by the Local Government Boundary Commission, my reason for the omission is one of convenience and not conviction.

There is here no need to catalogue the immense bibliography of books on Wales since the time of Pennant. Pennant himself and the later George Borrow, in spite of his prejudices, remain delightful and erudite observers, while among more recent contributions I would particularly single out *Beautiful Wales* by Edward Thomas, and *Wales* by Sir Owen M. Edwards. *The Welsh People*, written by Sir John Rhys and D. Brymor Jones late last century, remains a standard work, and *The Life and Opinions of Robert Roberts* is an invaluable portrait of Welsh life in the time of Queen Victoria. On more specialised subjects the following are admirable : *The Welsh*

*House*, by Iorwerth Peate ; *Welsh Folklore and Folk Custom*, by
T. Gwynn Jones ; *The Old Churches of Snowdonia* and *The Old
Cottages of Snowdonia*, both by Hughes and North ; *Tudor Policy
in Wales*, by J. F. Rees ; and *The Development of Welsh Poetry*, by
Sir Idris Bell.

I have drawn not a little from some of the above, and I am in-
debted to many people for their generosity, courtesy and informa-
tion, particularly to the following : Sir John Lloyd (Brecon), Pro-
fessor Gwyn Jones, Mr. Keidrych Rhys, Miss Lynette Roberts, the
Vicar of Margam, Mr. Albert Tilley, Mr. S. J. Garton, Mrs. Garnons
Williams, Sir William Goscombe John, R.A., Mr. John Cowper
Powys, Sir Frank Brangwyn, R.A., Mrs. Mary Gill, Mr. Mark
Sontag, and the Vicar of Mallwyd.

*Sutton Coldfield*                                      TUDOR EDWARDS.
*Autumn* 1949.

# CONTENTS

# ACKNOWLEDGMENT

THE Publishers wish to express their thanks to the following individuals and authorities for contributing illustrations to this volume. The Frontispiece is from a painting by Norman Janes reproduced by courtesy of Mr. J. V. Stephens of Reading; Fig. 48 is included by permission of the Lady Lever Gallery, Port Sunlight; Figs. 73 and 74 are from paintings in the National Gallery, by permission of the Trustees; Fig. 47 is included by courtesy of the National Library of Wales.

They must also thank the following photographers: Mr. P. B. Abery, Builth Wells, for Figs. 7 and 46; Messrs. Aerofilms, Ltd., for Figs. 14, 67 and 89; Mr. J. M. Brereton, Farnborough, for Fig. 2; British Railways (Western Region), for Fig. 8; Central Office of Information, for Fig. 103 (from a photo by J. Dixon-Scott); The Courtauld Institute of Art, for Figs. 61, 86, 87, 105, 106 and 107 (from photos by Mr. Fred H. Crossley, F.S.A.); Mr. G. Davies, Aberdare, for Figs. 4, 5, 11, 16 and 35; Mr. Herbert Felton, F.R.P.S., for Fig. 54; Messrs. Fox Photos, Ltd., for Fig. 85; Messrs. F. Frith & Co. Ltd., Reigate, for Fig. 19; Leonard and Marjorie Gayton, for Figs. 36, 38, 40, 69 and 77; Mr. E. Chambré Hardman, F.R.P.S., for Fig. 26; Mr. D. Jackson, Brecon, for Fig. 60; Mr. Shirley Jones, for Fig. 98; Messrs. Judges, Ltd., Hastings, for Figs. 24, 37, 50, 91 and 95; Mr. H. D. Keilor, for Figs. 29, 43 and 75; Mr. A. F. Kersting, F.R.P.S., for Figs. 49, 52, 55, 66, 84 and 90; Mr. Harry Meyer, Letchworth, for Figs. 30, 45 and 81; Mr. Llew E. Morgan, for Figs. 6, 20, 22, 23, 25, 42, 83 and 100; The Mustograph Agency, for Figs. 3, 15, 39, 41, 57, 72, 80, 101, 102 and 104; Mr. J. A. Pendlebury, for Figs, 62, 65 and 92; Messrs. Photo Union, Ltd., for Figs. 70 and 71; Mr. Walter Scott, Bradford, for Figs. 93 and 94; Messrs. W. H. Smith & Sons, Ltd., for Fig. 53; The Topical Press Agency, Ltd., for Fig. 99; Messrs. Raphael Tuck & Sons, Ltd., for Figs. 44, 51, 63, 76, 96 and 97 (from photos by the late Will F. Taylor), Mr. E. R. Forestier-Walker, for Figs. 27, 28 and 64; Miss M. Wight, for Fig. 21; Mr. Reece Winstone, A.R.P.S., for Figs. 31, 32 and 82.

# I

# INTRODUCTION: GEOLOGY TOPOGRAPHY CHARACTERISTICS

STANDING upon the windy belvedere of the ancient British camp that crowns the Malverns one may look westward, as Piers Plowman surely did, to a chequered and mountain-seamed land which seems as remote, as full of magic and illusion, as Tibet. And this vision, this ancient prospect is but enhanced if one selects a nearer bird's-eye view from anywhere in the highlands of the Marches, roughly on the line of Offa's Dyke. Westward lies this land of Wales, its deep valleys filled with shadows, its domed moorlands given over to hill-ponies and sheep, its quick-glinting rivers laving towns of antique beauty, its villages falling lazily about verdant slopes where sometimes the Moloch-like pit-heads are darkly silhouetted against the indented sky-line.

For all this, and more, is Wales. No area comparable in size is so complex in physical features, so rich in diversity of scenery, so steeped in history and antiquarian lore. Land of my Fathers she may be, but is she not feminine in visage and mood, or rather, perhaps, hermaphroditic? Protean in aspect she certainly is. I remember her as I saw her one severe winter when I tramped along the shores of the Carmarthen estuary and almost glissaded, wishing my boots had been studded with crampons, along the two miles of solid ice from Llanstephan to the remote village of Llanybri. I remember her as I saw her one autumn in the Black Mountains, when the mountainside was one great cascade of water and the Honddu was churned into a brown spate, a white, misty loneliness filling the valley; yet within five minutes I had been on sweet springing green lands warmed by a capricious sun. And thus I have seen her from the hamlet of Bryn Siencyn on Anglesey, looking across the spangled sun-shot strait to the massed *arêtes* of the Snowdon peaks, and, southward again, in the purlieus of the coalfields, looking across Cwm parc to the bruised rumps of Rhondda Fawr.

Geologically Wales is a mosaic of Pre-Cambrian and Cambrian rock, Ordovician and Silurian rock, Old Red and New Red sandstone, Car-boniferous limestone, Coal Measures and Millstone Grit. This in simpler interpretation more tangibly consists of slate, shale, granite, sandstone, limestone, coal, grit and sand, all of varying prehistoric ascendancy.

Their distribution over the face of Wales is widespread and often inter-locked. The high moorland plateau of central Wales is occupied by an outcrop of Ordovician and Silurian rock, and these beds of slate, shale and limestone cover parts of Carmarthen, Brecknock, Cardigan, Radnor and Montgomery. The oldest Pre-Cambrian rocks are confined to three areas, Anglesey, the Lleyn peninsula in Caernarvonshire and a small out-crop in north-west Pembroke. Anglesey itself is a parterre of varying strata about a nucleus of this Pre-Cambrian rock, and it is very evident that this lowland plain is no ordinary plain, but an ancient highland much reduced by erosion. The remainder of Caernarvon, and most of Merion-eth, is made up of Cambrian and Ordovician rock; the Harlech 'Dome' is the greatest mass of Cambrian rock in Britain, while Snowdon is Ordovician. In this area volcanic ashes and lava, mostly submarine, were transformed into the rhyolitic rocks that now clothe these moun-tains, though Snowdon itself was never a volcano. Pembroke is also largely composed of Cambrian and Ordovician strata.

There are two areas of sandstone or, more correctly, Marls, the Devonian seam of Old Red Sandstone which, coming from the English borders, passes through Brecknock and extends into south Pembroke, with a narrow projection into Carmarthen, and the New Red Sandstone or Trias which occupies the Vale of Clwyd in Denbighshire. This leaves the Coal Measures and Millstone Grits of Flint and Denbigh in the north and those extending across Glamorgan to the edge of Car-marthen in the south, the latter having a coastal fringe composed of Jurassic Lias, Triassic Red Marls and limestone.

This geological basis underlies a rich pattern of scenic landscape, a blend of the dramatic, Wild Wales indeed, and the more opulent softer textures. It is here more convenient to divide the Principality into its shires rather than into geological belts, such as the limestone, and we may pause to briefly examine their characteristics.

Glamorgan would seem to be paradoxical, for it is a quite remarkable compound of the agricultural and the industrial. It is a plateau watered by four main streams, the Rhondda, Taff, Neath and Tawe (the watershed of the last two extending into Brecknock), all of them largely harnessed to industry. The coalfield extends for some sixty miles over moorland mountain, and all the workings are within convenient distance of the ports of Newport, Cardiff, Barry, Swansea, etc. The relative importance of this coalfield has declined since the navy turned from smokeless coal to oil. The Rhondda valley is itself a compound comparable with the Ruhr basin in Germany, though the former is probably richer in iron ores. Coal-mining, copper smelting, and tin-plate work are responsible for the greatest density of population here, and Glamorgan has some fifteen hundred people to the square mile, and half the total population of Wales.

Yet there is rich loam soil in what is inaccurately termed the Vale of Glamorgan, and agriculture thrives in a much healthier state than one

2  SNOWDONIA LANDSCAPE.  Looking down on Llyn Eigiau from
Pen Llithrig-y-Wrach, Carnarvonshire

3   Glyn Ceiriog Valley, Denbighshire

might expect. Nor is it without significance that bananas are successfully grown about Swansea and that Margam possesses the finest Aleppo Pine in Britain. From Cardiff to Port Talbot there stretches a coastal plain rich in grazing pastureland and historic interest, while Gower is a peninsula with a magnificent limestone coast and a hinterland which is surprisingly remote. But it must be stressed that most of Glamorgan's best landscapes are to be found in the purlieus of the coalfields, in the northern region of the mountainous *Blaenau*.

Carmarthen is of a more pastoral character, well watered and wooded, its broad, open valleys and shamrock-green hills dotted with sheep and whitewashed cottages like Hebridean crofts. The Towy and its sweet infant Cothi flow into Carmarthen Bay, girdling the county town, the centre of national life in South Wales. Westward the Taf also meets the sea, its waters flowing beneath the ghostly creepered castle of Laugharne, while in the north-west the Teifi divides the shire from Cardigan. Eastward stretches the *massif* of the Black Mountains (52), the grim, cocoa-coloured corries of the Carmarthen Vans trespassing over the Brecknock border.

Pembroke occupies the south-west extremity of the country and is moderately fertile, its pastures supporting herds of Castlemartin black cattle. It is mainly watered by the east and west branches of the Cleddau, which unite with smaller streams below Haverfordwest to form the great harbour of Milford Haven. The coastline is heavily indented, and the magnificent scenery along the entire seaboard (31, 40, 41) reaches its acme in the basaltic rocks of the north coast, in the splintered, storm-swept shores of Dewisland and around St. Bride's Bay, with its creeks and fishing villages. Since Pembroke possesses sixteen major castles and over sixty *castellau*, it is known in cliché as The Land of Castles, but it is equally well known as The Land of the Flemings. Suggestions of a Flemish enclave may be seen in such survivals as the peculiar domestic architecture and the curious lug-sailed boats of Milford Haven. T. E. Lawrence was one of its devotees. He loved the green lands falling straight into the water, the cottage chimneys "as big as abutments" and the people who spoke "a beautiful soft English".

Cardigan too is a maritime shire with a long and attractive coast. The hinterland is largely agricultural—horse-breeding is one of its characteristics—with fine valleys along the courses of the rivers Teifi, Towy, Rheidol and Ystwyth, several of them quite dramatic and, especially in the north, pranked with coniferous trees. Plynlimon is the centre of a bog-overlaid shale plateau, and much of these northern uplands are remote and austere. I recall a lonely farm at the head of the Gogunan valley in winter and the desolate Tregaron Bog, which June swathes in cotton-grass.

Brecknock is girded about with its sister counties, except on its eastern perimeter, where it flirts with English Hereford and Monmouth. The red sandstone here assumes a monumental aspect in the Brecon Beacons (1, 50) and the heights of Pen-y-fan, recreational grounds of one of the

most beautiful of neglected towns.   The Black Mountains to the east are
softer and more capricious (52), though this hill country is sparsely
populated, for sheep farming is the rule.   To north and west are rolling
uplands which are largely agricultural, with a spate of chalybeate
and mineral springs and their attendant spas *manqués*.   The upper Wye
valley is wholly pastoral in character, framing a diadem of lovely villages on
its Brecknock southern bank, and the valley of the quick-glinting Usk has
an equal appeal, while the Tawe and smaller streams running southward
traverse moorlands of sombre and wild countenance, almost trackless save
for the Roman Sarn Helen across the curlew-frequented cotton-grass.

Neighbouring Radnor is the most sparsely populated county in Wales
(the logical extension of this is that adjacent Hereford stands in the same
relation to English shires).   The recesses of the treeless Radnor Forest are
given over to sheep-rearing, though not under the most favourable con-
ditions, and richer pastureland fringes the northern banks of the upper
Wye and Teme.   The northern wilderness, where the rare yellow moun-
tain-poppy grows, stretches away to Cwm Elan, now dammed with some
degree of artificial majesty.   Neighbouring Montgomery forms an
integral part of this same central tableland and has much the same
characteristics.   Its austere, peaty moorlands are fretted with deep valleys,
like that of the Pennant.   Sheep and Merlins, or Welsh mountain ponies,
roam the domed hills above the chequerwork of arable land below.   The
country is richly wooded, especially in the valley of the Severn, which,
rising east of Plynlimmon, flows with torrential force to Llanidloes, where
it is joined by the Clwyedog.   The scenery of the Dyfi and its tributaries in
the west compares favourably with the better-known landscapes of North
Wales.   Northward the humped-backed Moel Sych crowns the Berwyns,
while the triune peaks of the bold Breiddens dominate the north-east.

The remainder of North Wales, comprising Merioneth, Caernarvon,
Anglesey, Denbigh and Flint, may be divided up into the Plain of
Caernarvon and Anglesey, the Snowdon Forest, the Merioneth Mountains crowned by the white quartz peaks of Aran Mawddwy, Cader Idris,
the Halkin Mountains sired by Moel Fammau, and the Vale of Clwyd.

In Caernarvonshire erosion has made fairly nondescript the dwarfed
peaks of the Snowdon Forest, once in all probability of Alpine dimensions
and grandeur.   The semi-circular cups or arenas known as cirques which
were created when the glacier ice drifted away from the parent slopes,
usually at the head of a valley, are known in Wales as *cwms*, though they
are sometimes also referred to, as in Carmarthen, as corries, in the Scottish
manner.   The marks of glacial action are often very distinct, as in Cwm
Glas below Crib Goch on Snowdon.   Glaciers also excavated rock-basins,
and while most British lakes are not authentic rock-basins, the lakes of
Llydaw and Glaslyn and many a small mountain tarn are.

Snowdon has its own *genius loci* and has long been for the civilised
world the very personification of all Cymric tradition and legend, and

even now we persist in clothing it with some nebulous aura, much as the ancients regarded it as the home of immortal spirits, a kind of Valhalla. Mercifully we have ceased to associate it with those Emotions of Sublimity so fondly discussed in Georgian and even Victorian drawing-rooms. In sober fact most of our own generation regard it simply as a kind of Olympic training arena, and the Idwal slabs are more notorious for putting young rock-climbers through their baptism of fire than for anything else.

This area of Snowdonia is nicely sealed off by the Vales of Ffestiniog and Conway, which also conveniently mark the limits of Caernarvonshire. But there are two other aspects of this county to be considered. Westward points the long arm of the Lleyn peninsula, the *Canganorum promontorium* of Ptolemy, with its seafaring traditions, its Breton-like landscapes and its fertile tract of land sweeping around Tremadoc Bay. The other near-phenomenon is the slate country edging up to the Menai Strait. The slate quarries about Penrhyn are among the largest open-workings in Britain, their seventy-feet-high terraces piled one upon the other and all receding like the tiers of a Roman amphitheatre. (I once came upon one of these quarries in a winter's half-light, and it oddly resembled the rice terraces of the Philippines.)

Beyond the strait lies Anglesey, the Roman *Mona* of Tacitus and the cradle of the Tudor dynasty, its extensive cornfields and sacred groves now replaced by common and grazing land fenced in by stone walls and hedges of veronica. Later on we shall see that Anglesey is an island of neglected delights.

From the confines of Caernarvonshire a rich chequerwork of mountain, moorland and arable land is spread across Merioneth and Denbigh. Here are the softly tinted landscapes of David Cox, here the silver-threaded valleys of the Conwy, Llugwy, Lledr, Ceiriog, Dee and all their lovable, sparkling kith and kin. The watershed of the Berwyns forms the boundary between Merioneth, Denbigh and Montgomery. Eastward in Denbigh the hilly moorlands are relieved by the fertile, Cheshire-like Vale of Clwyd. A limestone belt runs along the edge of Denbigh and through Flint, where the Alyn, which begins as a thin moorland stream, carves its way through a deep gorge and separates the ore-seamed Halkin Mountains from the Clwydian range.

Geographically the most striking feature of the north, apart from the Snowdon Forest, is the Bala Cleft, the through way from the coast near Towyn on the western seaboard by the valley framing Lake Talyllyn to Lake Bala and along the valley of the Dee to the marsh flats of its estuary, with the ample Mawddach estuary (72) as a branch.

Such, very briefly, is the physical pattern of Wales. This alone has an obvious appeal, but when the pattern is embroidered with the woof and warp of the area, interwoven with the national life, it has an interest, pictorial and historical, social and cultural, on a parallel with that of larger

European communities of no less ancient lineage. Much romantic nonsense has been written about the Celt, invariably depicting him as an amorphous being, half genius, half lunatic; half saint, half devil. Pierre Loti painted such portraits for Brittany, Synge for Ireland, Quiller-Couch for Cornwall, and a few Welshmen (and women) have done the same thing for Wales, though the chief offenders have been Englishmen, like Theodore Watts-Dunton. I do not propose to add to such a portrait-gallery. Nor is this book concerned with history or economics except where they relate to subjects *en passant*.

Yet it *is* necessary to appreciate the Celtic inheritance or, more accurately, that sub-Celtic culture which lingers among the Welsh and the racial temperament inseparable from it (though authorities are divided upon the existence of the latter). Ethnological affinities can be traced between Wales and Ireland, Cornwall, the Hebrides, Brittany and parts of Switzerland and Spain. It is often asserted, with some degree of truth, that a Welshman speaking his own language in Brittany can make himself understood. Etymology apart, many a Breton small town has something of a Welsh countenance—Dol, for example, with its cobbled streets and granite houses. Here the people too have a Welsh cast of countenance, for these Armoricans are descendants from Britons of Wales and Dumnonia who sailed away in the fourth and fifth centuries, and the dark-grey, silvery granite cathedral of Dol owes its origin to St. Sampson and other early Welsh monks.

It was on the lowlands that fringe the coast of South Wales, and in the river valleys generally, that the earliest communities settled, and it is in these areas that the various successive culture phases, from the Neolithic to the Late Medieval, may be traced, made tangible for us in everything from the cromlech to the castle. And, significantly, these same areas are today the most densely populated in Wales. While some of the remote upland villages no doubt have their origin in early seasonal migration, movements up hill to the *Hafod* or summer pasture and down hill to the *Hendre* or permanent settlement in the valley with the approach of winter, much as isolated communities in parts of the Alps do today.

In rural life and husbandry survivals from early times may yet be seen though they are fast becoming museum-pieces. The peculiar bullock-cart used in Glamorgan until recent years was probably a survival in form of the ancient British chariot. Old looms and pandies, or woollen-mills, still function in many parts of the country; *cartheni*, or coloured, closely woven, reversible quilts and rugs, are peculiar to Wales and are yet sold in Carmarthen market, woven linseys and shawls are still worn, and it is evident that the Welsh had traditional plaids something like the Scottish tartans.

Sometimes the great Welsh Renaissance of the twelfth century seems but recent history, and passages in the *Mabinogion* and the *Itinerary* of Giraldus Cambrensis acquire more point, even a near-topical note. For we find coracles (43), the *vitilia navigia* of Pliny, on the Towy, Teify and

4   A Remote Chapel at Soar-y-Mynydd, Cardiganshire

5   The Village of Moelgrove, Cardiganshire

6   A Farmhouse Interior in Brecknockshire

7   Disserth Old Church, Radnorshire

Conwy, sycamore woodcarving in Cardigan, laver-bread in the south-west, liquors made from mountain-ash berries and birch sap, candles (*canwyll frwyn*) made from a plant growing in the marsh of Plynlimon, internal wells in houses; while it is said that on remote uplands Goidelic numerals are still in use for counting sheep. Many ritual gestures hark back to the Middle Ages. It is still possible to see in remote farmhouses a glass of water, a vase of flowers and a white tablecloth set, without any conscious motive, upon a bedroom table alongside the bed, a survival of the pre-Reformation viaticum ceremony.

A Welsh correspondent recently wrote me lamenting and puzzling the fact that "architectural taste in Wales, amongst a people so completely charmed with poetry and music, is so low and rudimentary". The problem is posed, not solved. No doubt the post-Reformation wave of evangelical puritanism and the long years of political and economic subjection have been contributing factors. Certainly the mass-production of slates, red and yellow pressed bricks and vitrified bricks, which began towards the middle of last century, finally choked the breath out of architecture in the Principality. We are, however, casting stones from the insecure shelter of glass-houses, for these remarks also apply in large measure to England today.

There is, of course, no *Welsh* architecture, though there is a modest domestic architecture which is a sub-Celtic survival; one has but to indicate the 'longhouse' and *croglofft*.[1] Regional characteristics include the peculiar cottage architecture around St. David's, with the massive round chimneys and baking-ovens popularly dubbed Flemish, but more probably sub-Norman, the pitched and patterned cobbled floors of Montgomery, the tiled floors of Brecknock, and the circular pigsties of Glamorgan and elsewhere, those picturesque swineries which have Irish, Scottish and Gaulish characteristics, but which also recall native homesteads in the Krongo hills of the Nubian Mountains. The timber-frame tradition overflows from Cheshire, Shropshire and Hereford into Denbigh, Montgomery and Radnor, while in south and mid-Wales there are white-harled stone cottages, often colour-washed, with thatched roofs. The art and use of thatch has declined, not only because of mass-production of more durable materials but also because Welsh cornfields are not so extensive as formerly. Anglesey has a monopoly of granite, but while stone of all kinds is a common medium, there is too often the raw, blatant ugliness of the now ubiquitous brick and slate.

The castle is obviously of a different and wholly scientific *genre*, but it is notable that Edward I, who was responsible for the ring of fortress towns in the north, served his apprenticeship amid the *bastides* of Gascony and was a forerunner of modern town-planners. Nor do we meet with town-planning again in Wales until we reach Tremadoc in the early

[1] These have been admirably dealt with by Dr. Iorwerth Peate in his *The Welsh House*.

nineteenth century.  Some half-hearted measures, it is true, were adopted during the preceding century at Aberystwyth, Montgomery, Brecon, Aberayron and elsewhere (there is some excellent Georgian architecture in the Principality), while an early Victorian example is Beaumaris on the Menai Strait, largely built by the Lancashire-born Joseph Hansom for his patron, Lord Bulkeley.  Post-Reformation architecture and craftsmanship in Wales are almost wholly the work of Englishmen commissioned by a Welsh squirearchy (though John Nash, Sir Uvedale Price, the Davies brothers, John Gibson, Pritchard of Llandaff and Sir William Goscombe John belong to this area).

The country is no less rich in ecclesiastical architecture than in castles, manor-houses, crosses, etc., though there is not the opulence that abounds in the historic prosperity of English parishes (their church-livings now less plump than formerly).  The more remote uplands contain Celtic and sub-Celtic survivals, invariably severe buildings with plain gables and bell-cotes, some on the double-cube plan, and often preserving early Christian arrangements reminiscent of the Abyssinian Copts.  It is in the hill country too that those later medieval churches rich in rood-screens and other carved woodwork will be found.  Among other regional characteristics there are the twin-naved churches of Denbighshire (at Llangwnadl in the Lleyn is a church with the Cornish or Kent type of three equal naves, each separately roofed and gabled), the low towers with simple or multi-staged pyramidal roofs or small wooden turrets found about the Marches, the quasi-military church towers and saddle-backs of Glamorgan, and the good local craftsmanship of the fourteenth century in Pembroke and the south-west, part of a movement designed and stimulated by Bishop Gower in his diocese of St. David's.

But, above all, Wales is rich in human beings and human resources, and the peculiar native genius cannot be flatly contained within a *Dictionary of National Biography*.  Once on the western side of Offa's Dyke and the lyrical element in humanity becomes more pronounced, for the Welsh are a poetic people—poetic, that is, in their reaction to life, to love and death, to joy and suffering.  It would be fatuous to regard every Welshman as an embryo poet, yet it is probably true that the proportion of poets per population is greater here than in any other country.  Here men still gather to read poetry aloud, as they did in the Paris of Mallarmé, the Dublin of George Moore and, for a brief space, the London of the eighteen-nineties, though here there is a little less blarney.

Music, poetry, hospitality, a love of words and language and a flair for education are some of the characteristics contributing to the very real individuality of the Welsh, and this is as true of the miners of Rhondda as it is of the coracle-makers of Cenarth, the laver-gathers of Freshwater Bay, the drovers of Tregaron, the ballad-making, sheep-rearing farmers of Montgomery, the fishermen of Aberdaron and the innkeeper-mountain guide-philosophers of the Snowdon Forest.

8   The Mumbles Lighthouse, Glamorganshire

9   St. Donat's Castle, Glamorganshire

10   Cardiff Castle

*Both from Paul Sandby's "View in . . . Wales" (1775)*

# II

## CARDIFF  THE RHONDDA VALLEY
## THE VALE OF GLAMORGAN

IT might be as well to begin any perambulation of South Wales from Cardiff, a city of neglected delights and one sufficiently 'foreign' in texture and atmosphere as to be both intriguing and stimulating. For in spite of its nationalist institutions and its murmurs of bilingual speech, this city has a cosmopolitan air second only to that of London. Its castle has a great tower like a German *Schloss* and its civic centre, in Cathays Park, one of the modern wonders of the Western world, has an exuberance, a flamboyancy of sculpture that is eminently Latin and puts my Parisian friends at their ease. The many units comprising this aldermanic pleasance were all designed by different architects, and indeed the only common denominators are the pristine Portland stone and the closely cropped swards. The architecture is largely hybrid, combining the entire gamut of the Classical orders with the functional *motifs* of the twentieth century. Yet collectively here is a truly splendid vision of what this century might have been before it entered the realm of prefabs and aesthetic liquidation. One would single out for special attention the National Museum of Wales, a model of what museums should be; the City Hall, with a lofty tower that seems to have been taken from the cathedral of Caracas in Venezuela; the War Memorial, by J. N. Comper, who for once has departed from his Gothic *milieu* and with marked success; and, in general, the sculpture of the Cardiff-born Sir William Goscombe John.

It is a caustic commentary on officialdom that Cardiff Castle (10) is more difficult of access now that it belongs to the city corporation than when the Marquesses of Bute lived in it. Yet it is worth while penetrating beyond the vast coffee- and henna-coloured enceinte walls of this fairy-tale castle, largely a Victorian fantasy by that William Burges who wallowed in the thirteenth-century Gothic of France. Burges recast the entire east face of the castle, adding the effective if incongruous machicolated clock-tower and skilfully restoring the whole. In internal decoration his medievalism ran riot; there are tiles and ogee arches everywhere, the banqueting hall has a fireplace like the castellated entrance to a railway tunnel, and there is a Chaucer Room and an Arab Room, the former filled with mural paintings and stained glass depicting *The Canterbury Tales*. A few stones of the Roman *castrum Tibia Amnis*, on which the castle was originally built, survive in the enceinte, and the old *motte* is crowned with an impressive shell of a thirteenth-century polygonal keep.

Just eastward of the castle are the thirteenth-century foundations of a Franciscan church with the nondescript ruin of a manor-house built on the friary site at the Dissolution. In the town-centre is the parish church of St. John, mainly fifteenth-century, its excellent tower, of West-Country type, having stone latticed louvers, enriched parapet and crocketed pinnacles. Internally there are early-Renaissance parclose screens combining Gothic and near-Jacobean ornament and an effective altar-piece by Goscombe John.

These provide the sum-total of the city's pre-Reformation buildings. It is quite remarkable that beyond castle, church and friary Cardiff has no architecture earlier than the beginning of the last century. Its oldest house of any pretensions is a modest one of *c.* 1800 in Working Street, and even here the admirable Roman Doric convex porch of wood has been removed to the museum. Old Cardiff was rebuilt under the second Marquess of Bute during the last century even more thoroughly than was Birmingham under Joseph Chamberlain, and there is surprisingly little by way of pictorial illustration to show us what the city was like, nothing in fact earlier than Paul Sandby's water-colours (10), with the single exception of an engraving by the Buck brothers of 1748. This latter gives no more than a meagre hint of former riches. There was an intriguing Town Hall of 1747, with Dutch gable and cupola and two flights of steps flanking a double-decker entrance, and there was the early-Stuart Red House, later the Cardiff Arms Inn, which had an excellent staircase contained within a central square tower.

For the rest, there is a typical Bodley church at Roath Park, the Edgbaston of Cardiff, while only the bomb-cauterised shell remains of the R.C. Cathedral of St. David, an interesting Victorian church of the open college-hall type. Yet this is an airy, spacious city of noble vistas, of pleasances and gardens, of graving docks and steel works, of ample streets in which the ubiquitous Ruskinian Gothic of England is for once refreshingly absent. The respectable suburb of Canton belies its name, and China is more apt to be found in the purlieus of Bute Street and the docks, the *Tiger Bay* of modern fiction, a cesspool of Asiatic lodging-houses and chop-suey cafés where one may come across a house with Greek candle-lit shrine flaring in the living-room.

Llandaff, now almost a suburb of Cardiff, adjoins the bungaloid settlement of Whitchurch. Its cathedral, half-hidden below its sheltering ridge, was probably founded by St. Teilo in the sixth century. For a small church it has both beauty and majesty, and it is unique among ancient cathedral churches in its lack of transepts, triforium and vaulted roof.

Fragments of Norman fabric remain in the presbytery, with its magnificent Romanesque arch, and in two entrances into the nave, but the structure is mainly Decorated work of varying periods. The exceptions are the rather singular chapter-house, Early English, with an octagonal roof added by Pritchard, and the massive north-west tower, late fifteenth-century and of West Country inspiration. By the beginning of the eighteenth century neglect had made a ruin of the cathedral, and John Wood was called in to restore the structure. Wood's customary genius as displayed at Bath here eluded him, and the 'Italian temple' which he created was a travesty. Mercifully, in 1842 John Pritchard, son of a vicar-choral of Llandaff, was appointed as architect. Pritchard's work had a tendency towards the 'streaky bacon' styles of Butterfield and Woodward, but his restoration of Llandaff was executed in an earlier tradition and bore the fruit of his training under the elder Pugin. It was distinguished by an admirable restraint, but was given a touch of whimsy in a new tower and spire which savours more of Normandy than ot Glamorgan and is in fact reminiscent of St. Pierre at Caen. This tower was the most striking feature of Llandaff, but it is now truncated, while the entire building is a gloomy empty shell. Bombs do not discriminate about such things, and the smashing of Llandaff was a major tragedy.

Near the village green, with its cross marking, it is said, the spot from which Archbishop Baldwin preached the Third Crusade, as described by Giraldus Cambrensis, are the remains of the original episcopal palace, a rectangular shell with angle towers and early fourteenth-century gate-house, destroyed by Owen Glyndowr in 1402. The new palace is a severe symmetrical building of c. 1751, with a fragment of a ninth-century Celtic wheel-head cross on the lawn.

From Llandaff a road follows the valley of the tiny Ely, with its monkshood flowers, to St. Fagan's. This village is dominated by St. Fagan's Castle, a sixteenth-century multi-gabled house with buttressed central porch wing on the site of a thirteenth-century castle, and from the foot of the hill has a rather dramatic aspect, the castle overhanging the thatched, white-harled cottages and the railway in startling proximity. St. Fagan's provided until quite recently an interesting example of feudal tenure, all the villagers being retainers of the Earls of Plymouth and having a high percentage of incipient madness through inbreeding, while even upon a villager's death the coffin was made on the estate. Thus it seems a singularly happy choice for the National Museum of Wales to have chosen this estate for the site of a Welsh folk-museum, potentially a large show piece with reconstructed Welsh houses, farm, workshops of native crafts-men—turner, stone-mason, weaver, carpenter, smith, potter, etc.—on the lines of the great open-air folk-museum at Skansen in Sweden.

Meanwhile the nucleus of this museum already exists in the castle itself, furnished with exhibits of various dates drawn from Welsh manor-houses. The latter include, *inter alia*, Flemish tapestries, early-nineteenth-century furniture from Coed Coch in Denbighshire, a triple harp and a wig stand. The grounds, with leaden figures of fiddler and piper looking out over the terraced gardens, distinctly recall the layout at Powys Castle in Welshpool. Parapets of terraces and walls have arabesque treatment, while the Elizabethan herb garden, mulberry garden, Georgian pigeon-cote and fishponds complete a gracious picture.

On the eastern perimeter of Cardiff, entering the village of St. Mellons, which is just in Monmouth, and crossing the Rhymney river back into Glamorgan, one finds Cefn Mably on its wooded hill. Now a hospital, this historic house is said to have been originally built by Mably (Mabel), daughter and heiress of Robert Fitzhamon, Earl of Gloucester, about the year 1150. There is nothing of the original, but a much-restored six-teenth-century wing contains a Long Gallery with plain plaster barrel roof and an artfully contrived priest's chamber leading down to the river. The Queen Anne wing, in the Wren tradition, was built for that Sir Charles Kemeys who refused to attend the Court of George I, though he had often visited him in Hanover, intimating that while he had been ready to smoke a pipe with George as Elector of Hanover, he would not with George as King of England. This south-east front is a charming ten-windowed range, all the windows in arched architraves and all preserving their original glazing-bars. The cream-pilastered porch has a small pediment with urns as acroteria, there is a coved plaster eaves cornice and a roof nicely broken up by nine moulded wood dormers. The main hall has coeval furnishing, but the Queen Anne panelling conceals some of over a century earlier. The house, mantled with magnolia, stands in a Poussin landscape of mulberry trees, oaks and others all dominated by a giant cedar.

From nearby Ruperra Castle, a quadrangular shell of *c.* 1600 with an interior of 1789, one can reach Caerphilly road. The town, with its locomotive works, collieries and stone quarries, is set in a magnificent natural amphitheatre between the hills through which winds the broad valley of the Rhymney. The presiding spirit of Caerphilly frowns from the castle (11), which thrusts its will upon the half-acquiescent town, dominating the stuccoed houses of the market-place and rising against the green-domed Caerphilly Mountain. This is the largest military ruin in all Britain, the first of the concentric fortresses of the Edwardian type and an ingenious work having three main lines of defence, seven gate-houses and some thirty portcullises. T. E. Lawrence wrote that "It pollutes it to mention any (castles) but Château Gaillard, Pembroke and Caerphilly in the same breath" (i.e. as Fougères in France), though his fervour would probably have waned over Caephilly's now largely restored state. Among its many original features are the revetted horn-work on the west, the *tête-du-pont* and the massive screen wall, heavily buttressed on one side and sustained by three towers on the other, a remarkable work of military engineering. The castle was begun in 1267,

11   Caerphilly Castle, Glamorganshire (c. 1270)

12, 13   Llantwit Major, Glamorganshire
The Medieval Cross of Houelt, and Jesse Niche

14   Castell Coch, Glamorganshire.   An air view of the much-restored Castle

though it is almost certain that the concentric works are slightly later, but in spite of the pains taken to make it the most impregnable fortress in the country, it passed through few vicissitudes and was never besieged more severely than during the milky foray by Queen Isabella's barons; its only humiliation was its deliberate 'slighting' by gunpowder in the seventeenth century.

Caerphilly has little else to show. Robert Oldmeadow in a piquant essay has already indicated that Caerphilly cheese is no more, or rather that what remains of it is now manufactured in alien Leicester. Watford Chapel, however, has much status among nonconformists, for here were held those services which resulted in the union of Welsh and English Methodism. It was founded in 1662, but was subsequently rebuilt, and now presents the nondescript appearance common to all of this ilk. George Whitefield, that sexual neurotic who had always found in himself nothing more than "a fitness to be damned", but who in spite of this launched Calvinistic Methodism, stayed in the district and was married here; and in a cottage on the mountainside was born David Williams, who drafted the first constitution of the French Revolution, founded the Royal Literary Fund, met Voltaire, and sheltered Benjamin Franklin from persecution. The harpists of Caerphilly have been celebrated, and the Welsh National Anthem was written by two local brothers.

From Caerphilly a by-road crosses the mountains to meet the Cardiff–Pontypridd road at Nantgarw, home of a lost porcelain of great *éclat*. From here it is worth while doubling back as far as Taff's Well, passing the new Treforest Trading Estate which recalls the Great West Road out of London. Just beyond Taff's Well the red dolomite, conical-capped towers of Castell Coch (14) are perched on the wooded hillside overlooking the Taff. This is another joint creation of William Burges and that Marquess of Bute who translated the Roman Breviary and several Coptic rites and who was the original of Disraeli's *Lothair*. It is a *petit* fort of the Gibbs' 'Ivory Castle' *genre*, triangular, with drum-towers at each angle. Originally built in the thirteenth century to guard the narrow pass of the valley, it is plausibly restored externally, somewhat on the lines of Viollet-le-duc's restoration of Carcassonne, though the panel above the gateway, with its relief of the Madonna against a sea-blue background diapered with fleurs-de-lis, strikes a new and lyrical note. The courtyard has wooden allures corbelled out on its curtain wall and recalls Tretower in Brecknock. Internally there is a wealth of fresco by Burges, and the octagonal Drawing-room is a near-replica of the Chaucer Room at Cardiff, though the allegorical subjects patterned on the walls are different, but it is a garish effort, overdressed with lunettes, balustrades and a dome-like vault supported on cornucopia corbels.

The sluggish Taff may be followed to Pontpridd, sitting astride the river at the head of the smoking valleys, at the head of the area of the Great Depression though not of it. Indeed, Pontypridd has charms enough for any week-ender wishing to escape to an ivory tower. There is the miniature tableland of the common with its ancient *Maen Chwf* or rocking-stone, its modern Druidic circle, spurious as the Gorsedd itself, and the white round houses built and lived in by William Price of Llantrisant, one of the most colourful eccentrics of the last century, medico, *soi-disant* Archdruid of Wales, instigator of Chartist riots, political refugee in France, pioneer of cremation (he soaked his own son's body in paraffin and, Abraham-like, burned it on a mountain-top), rake and father to a host of illegitimates. There is the Garth Mountain, lovely with its beeches in autumn, the Eglwysilan Mountain with its ancient chapel, whinberry-gathering on the Graig and bird-nesting in the quarry. Do the boys still plunge into the canal locks for wagers, I wonder, as they did when I was a child? Then, in the town there is William Edwards' bridge, in its time a wonder, for its single span excelled that of the Rialto in Venice. Since Edwards was minister as well as engineer, he was known as 'Bridge Builder for Both Worlds', and he was summoned to the Court of Catherine of Russia, a singular honour (though he declined it), to be shared with the French Clérisseau, the Scottish Cameron and William Hollins of Birmingham.

The constant vilifying of the Rhondda Valley has become a noxious habit. Certainly the squalor associated with technological achievement, with exploitation and unemployment is much in evidence. The towns are for the greater part mean, drab creations, each with its terraces of papier-maché houses piled higgledy-piggledy on the gashed mountainside, each with its Victorian neo-Gothic church designed by Pritchard or that John Norton who worked in Somerset, each with its clan of Dissenting tabernacles. These chapels, a few of them of good original design, are in the main an unoffending, prosaic lot, each closed to a six-day secular world and filled with the Sabbath *hwll* of some local Boanerges, though John Piper has shown that they can be subjects for an artist. Yet perhaps we would not have them otherwise, for they are collectively the only folk-architecture in the Principality and the very essence of Welsh life.

Sometimes the surface of the river which fills the narrow tortuous valley is veiled with scum and the moulting trees are ringed with coal dust. Artificial mountains spawned from slag sprawl in a carnal embrace over the bellies of the legitimate mountains. In the towns there are undertones of poverty relieved by great effort and courage. There is the black-faced minstrelsy of miners, like some sub-human—or superhuman—race apart, on furlough from the grudging earth. The *shonis* of my childhood have all but vanished. Undoubtedly this is an environment that breeds and fosters militant Socialism. On the roads between the pit-heads and the tightly packed homesteads solemn young men debate politico-sociology, and with an *ex cathedra* air, declare that once and for all "We must completely eliminate the bourgeoisie". By all means if it will serve any useful purpose, but *à quoi bon*?

This is not the romantic north. There is little traditional growth here and history has barely begun. What history there is is the history of evangelicalism, agitation, industry and sport. Richard Llewellyn is a more sensitive artist than Jack Jones, but for all that the true Rhondda is more apt to be found in the latter's *Rhondda Roundabout* than in the former's *How Green was my Valley*. One has the romantic vision and the other has the more prosaic but more accurate eye of the journalist.

Yet physically this is an area infinitely less spoiled than its English Black Country counterparts. It is possible to walk in about ten minutes from any pit-head into deep cwms, to wander over virgin hillsides and beside crystal-clear streams. There is always the scenic background, always the eternal mountains, especially above Tonypandy, scene of the riots of 1910, Treorchy, where the mountain road to Aberavon looks inviting, but above all beyond Treherbert and about the ancient shrine of Penrhys. That such an area, in spite of its teeming industrial communities, has remote fastnesses may be gauged from the fact that Llanwonno church, on the mountain road from Ynysybwl to Ferndale between the Rhondda and Aberdare valleys, claims to be the loneliest in all Wales.

The Aberdare valley is wider and greener than grim Rhondda, and Aberdare itself is not typical of the valley communities. Except for the shafts and rail-heads of the Navigation Collieries, the land sweeps north-westward clean and bright. The town has a more stable note, even a hint of prosperity in its early nineteenth-century rusticated buildings, its architraves about the windows and its Conservative Club like a miniature French Renaissance palace. And here, at Maesydref, one may meditate upon the complexities of a French Gothic church designed by English architects (including Thomas Hardy) and devoted to Welsh services. The missel-thrush comes to Aberdare. Indeed it is possible to see Aberdare with the eyes of a poet, as Alun Lewis saw it.

But it is time to be moving westward across that lush green terrain erratically known as the Vale of Glamorgan. The confines of the Vale are vague and conflicting, but in general they may be accepted as stretching, east to west, from somewhere about Kenfig to Penarth and, north to south, from the foothills of the mountain range to the coast. The long single street of Cowbridge makes a good pushing-off place. This is probably the Roman *Bovium* and is, or was, a medieval walled town strangely isolated from its castle. It is also known in cliché, I fail to see why, as the Cranford of Glamorgan. There are a few interesting houses, mainly of *c.* 1800, though many of the façades conceal earlier fabric. The early nineteenth-century town hall, formerly a house of correction, is a high-pitched building with arched treatment, clock-tower and cupola. The Duke Inn is an attractive Georgian pub of whitewashed stone. Near the modern grammar school, of Elizabethan foundation, is the only remaining town gate, its military air somewhat matched by the parish church's unusual octagonal tower parapet of thirteenth-century date.

Across the fields lies Llanbleiddian, sheer Cotswold in its dramatic siting and remote air, its whitewashed cottages perched on hillside terraces, its orchards and its brook-like Thaw tumbling and gurgling over weirs and beneath footbridges.    This is Carlyle's "little sleeping cataract of white houses", and here lived Carlyle's friend, John Sterling, pioneer among journalistic military commentators.    The church has a plain tower of West-Country character and a trefoiled piscina, and the small fourteenth-century castle ruin retains a fragment of what must have been an elaborate gatehouse.    The miniature valley of the Thaw in its brief life between here and the coast contains the relics of several castles, all of them modest and largely architectural palimpsests, chief of which are Beaupré, which is really an Elizabethan mansion with an effective porch combining Palladian and Gothic, and Fonmon, where a small rectangular Norman keep is concealed by later additions, mostly Jacobean.

From Llanbleiddian the bramble-hemmed lane, occasionally pranked with wild clematis, that leads to Llantwit Major looks inviting, climbing until panoramic views of the Vale are revealed on both sides and then dropping into the hamlet of Llanvihangel.    Here manor-house and church, and there is nothing else, both greying and brooding, stand on opposite sides of a dell reputedly haunted by the ghost of one of the chatelaines who lived at the manor.    The house itself is sixteenth-century, castellated, with mullioned windows, a gabled angle projection and a crenellated tower, and its hall has yet an enriched coved and quarried plaster ceiling and a fireplace with emblazoned overmantel.    There is an air of melancholy decrepitude about this lonely house which is intensified by the gaunt church with saddlebacked tower, corbelled parapet and near-*meurtrières*.

Llantwit, like Llancarfan not far distant, was one of the early cradles of Celtic Christendom.    The monastery was founded by the Breton St. Iltyd, who died *c.* 540, and among a coterie of celebrated saints who received instruction here were Gildas, the historian; Sampson, Archbishop of Dol; Paulinus, Bishop of Leon; Paul Aurelian; and possibly St. David himself (who, strangely enough, may never have been canonised at all). Though the monastic school was celebrated, the monastery was probably little more than one of those *monasteriola*, or 'petty monasteries', on the lines of the *coenobium* of St. Pachiomus rather than the earlier *laura* of St. Basil.    Late in the eleventh century Llantwit was reduced to penury for the benefit of Tewkesbury Abbey by the Norman Robert Fitzhamon, lackey of William the Conqueror, who dominated Glamorgan and who was mortally wounded in the siege of Falaise.

What remains of this monastery, or rather its successor, is a church of exceptional interest set in a churchyard which is a romantic rose garden. It consists of two adjoining churches, the western church, mainly a fifteenth-century rebuilding of the Norman church, with the ruins of a thirteenth-century Galilee chapel, and the eastern church or thirteenth-

15  Neath Abbey, Glamorganshire
Forlorn fragments of a twelfth-century foundation

16  St. John's Church, Aberdare, Glamorganshire

17   Ewenny Priory, Glamorganshire
The Screen and Norman South Transept from the Choir

century extension. The whole is rich in all the minutiae beloved of ecclesiologists (12, 13) and contains, *inter alia*, a fourteenth-century reredos, a beautifully carved niche with the sleeping figure of Jesse, thirteenth-century work and possibly part of the original altar-piece, a coeval mural painting of Mary Magdalene in red robe and flowing head-dress, an almost-Dutch abundance of good engraved ledger stones, some with variants of floriated crosses and fleurs-de-lis, and a collection of early Celtic pillars and cross-shafts with inscriptions and knot and interlaced work.

In the town, jostling the colour-washed cottages in the narrow winding streets, are two inns, the Swan and the White Hart, with mullioned fenestration of the fifteenth century. The town hall is largely of this period, with identical fenestration, a gabled façade with bell-cote and a peculiar projection containing steps to the upper storey. The early sixteenth-century small house is fairly common in the Vale, but a number of them in and about Llantwit have lately been allowed to fall into ruin. The fact that there exists in a meadow north of the town a Roman villa with mosaic pavements comparable with those at Chedworth, earthed over within living memory and now almost unknown, provides yet another measure of the apathy and philistinism of our time.

Beyond the road that skirts the coast lies St. Donat's with its castle snugly tucked away in a glen filled with myrtles and sub-tropical trees (9). The castle, of the concentric type, is inhabited, indeed it boasts that it has never been otherwise, but little of the original structure remains, though its fourteenth-century nucleus with Elizabethan and Stuart additions and the Victorian pruning and armorial stonework by the fastidious Bodley make of it a noble house, rich in aesthetic *curiosa*, Grinling Gibbons work and a singular ceiling of moulded copper. The Stradlings, a notable Marcher family, held it until 1738, when the last male heir was killed in a duel in France while making the Grand Tour. His body was brought to St. Donat's, where it lay in state, but the flambeaux surrounding the coffin caught some of the furniture and all but destroyed the picture-gallery. The recent acquisition of the castle by an American millionaire has safeguarded the property, but has made it rather less plausible, on account of a tendency to give it some Hollywood colour and to make it a potting-shed for antique houses, panelling, etc., uprooted from many an English landscape, including the newly sited remains of Bradenstoke Abbey from Wiltshire. The seventeenth-century ruins of a cavalry barracks, this *in situ*, standing between the glen and the sea strike a bizarre note.

The parish church, set in feudal juxtaposition with the castle, has another of the inescapable fortified Norman towers, horrific gargoyles, a font with the scale decoration found at Llantwit, a pre-Reformation altar with the consecration crosses visible on the *mensa*, a French Renaissance *ambon* or pulpit of wood, richly carved (this may be a reproduction;

3**

I have forgotten) and a lady-chapel of which the centre is filled by an altar tomb of 1740, where lies the young and impetuous duellist, an unusual honour for such a late monument. The churchyard cross is one of those calvaries of the Breton and Cornish type which are more numerous in the south than in the north, and this one has its original fifteenth-century head with carvings of the Crucifixion and a crowned Virgin.

Between St. Donat's and St. Bride's Major—from where, about the middle of last century, there was a large-scale exodus to Salt Lake City and the delights of Mormon hetaerism—lies a group of villages of some interest. There is Marcross, with a rude Norman church with later saddlebacked tower, at the head of a wooded valley leading down to the treacherous Nash sand-bank and the black-and-white banded lighthouses, Monknash with stone-tiled church (its timber roof reputedly made from wrecked Spanish Armada vessels) and remains of a monastic grange, and Wick with old malthouses and another saddlebacked church. From the hill-set village of Wick, with its plantations of chestnuts, one can strike southward to the coast, to sandy Dunraven Bay and Southerndown, which is walled by high cliffs of interesting geological formation, the strata of lias and carboniferous limestone laid one upon the other. Overlooking the headland is Dunraven Castle, nineteenth-century pastiche with castellated walls and pinnacles, set in a deer park.

The area beyond St. Bride's is best explored from Bridgend, a market town upon the Ogmore which has little to commend it beyond the ruin of a late twelfth-century castle with a remarkable gatehouse and the early Decorated church of St. Iltyd. On Newcastle Hill is an interesting sixteenth-century house, now derelict, which may have been a hospice of the Knights of St. John of Jerusalem, and at the top of the hill is the Georgian Newcastle House and a vicarage embodying some medieval work. For the rest, there is a Greek Doric market hall with tetrastyle portico, an indifferent Baptist Chapel of 1795 and a number of bridges, only one ancient, across the Ogmore. Several important excursions may be made from here. At Coity across the common land is one of the best examples of the 'ring' castle, or castle with a single and inner ward which originally consisted of a banked and ditched enclosure. The existing structure is a composite one: the keep and curtain wall are late twelfth-century, the former later enlarged, while an outer ward was added in the fourteenth century, there is a handsome later round tower of three storeys jutting into the moat to provide cross-fire across the curtain, and a Tudor chimney dominates the fourteenth-century hall, chapel and kitchens. The fine cruciform church, mainly fourteenth-century, has a vaulted tower crossing, trefoiled piscinae, cinquefoiled sedilia and a late-medieval saddlebacked oak coffer enriched with the emblems of the Passion. Coychurch, to the west, has an even more imposing church, with plain but elegant façade containing lobed quatrefoil windows diamond-shaped within, a single-sided cinquefoiled clerestory, a peculiar blank bay before the crossing, a handsome fifteenth-century wagon roof, and all the original chancel accessories.   But ecclesiology apart, the district contains such mild excitements as a megalithic chambered tomb of the long cairn type and a derelict house with wall panels carved with representations of spade, club, diamond and heart, locally believed to have been a gambling-house.

The Ewenny stream, rich in grayling where it is not poisoned by garbage, flows just south-eastward of Bridgend, and lying darkly upon its bank is Ewenny Priory, one of the most important examples of a fortified ecclesiastical building in the country.   The hoary ruins of what remain of the domestic buildings look more like castle than monastery, with a heavily spurred gatehouse having *meurtrières* and the *mashe-coulis* so familiar in French medieval illustrations.   The priory was a Benedictine foundation of the early twelfth century, becoming shortly afterwards a cell of Gloucester.   The church (17) now consists of nave, central tower, south transept and monastic choir and presbytery separated from the parochial nave by a stone *pulpitum*.   The massive piers and the chevron and scallop mouldings are typical of their pious but gory age, and a nicely arcaded gallery forming a quasi-triforium in the transept gives the only hint of caprice in this severe ensemble, in which even the fenestration is reduced to a minimum.   There are some excellent medieval sepulchral slabs, including that of the founder, Maurice de Londres, *obit.* 1149, with a floriated cross and Lombardic inscription.   Part of the monastic enceinte is occupied by an equally severe Georgian mansion.

In the vicinity of Ewenny is a pottery which has been working since at least the seventeenth century and is one of the comparatively few village crafts surviving in Wales.   Much of the ornamental reddish-brown earthenware produced here during the eighteenth and early nineteenth centuries was of Celtic inspiration; certainly the most fascinating of these products were the wassail-bowls of a highly festive character, which were used in connection with the *Mari Lwyd* festivities.   Today works of traditional slip-ware are still produced by the older methods.

The Ewenny stream skirts a road fringed with poppies and celandines until it joins the Ogmore river, and near the confluence of these waters stands the whitened shell of Ogmore castle, with one of the rare rectangular keeps of the south.   The appeal of this place, however, is purely pastoral.   The castle stands on the river bank against a background of forest and what appears to be a glacier of sand falling down from a miniature Alp of sand-dunes.   From here one crosses the stepping-stones to the opposite bank and the sweet hamlet of Merthyr Mawr.   Should the river be in spate then cross higher up by the medieval bridge with parapets arranged for sheep-washing.   Merthyr Mawr is an idyll of woodland, glen and thatched stone cottages, each with mullioned windows, chamfered arches, corbelled-out chimneys and, in one case, an external stone staircase to the upper floor.   The big house is a Regency mansion of no particular merit, though creamy and sun-lit and having among its adjuncts a bamboo forest; and in the churchyard of the neat Victorian Gothic church with its candle-extinguisher bell-cote is another original calvary with restored cross-head.

A sweet-smelling lane nods at grey farmyard and sleeping collies and then cautiously avoids the billowing sand-dunes until it gives it up and becomes hopelessly lost in the wilderness. For some way these dunes are screened by poplars, with a riot of bracken and giant fern-fronds in the immediate foreground. The sand-blown ruin of Candleston Castle, a fifteenth-century fortified manor-house, its fireplaces yet decorated with rosettes and pilastered shafts, seems to be the last outpost in this windswept, apricot-coloured desert. Stories of quicksands may be ignored. I struck a way across a landscape which was reminiscent of the sand-dunes about Schoorl in northern Holland and came out of a luxuriant dingle to climb to Candleston Farm and cross a hill-top with stone-built sheep-dipping pond. Northward the tower of Laleston church rose brightly, thrusting upward against the folds of the sombre hills.

On the road beyond Candleston Farm, and the way thence is a tres-passer's cross-country walk, lies Tythegston, its court of *c.* 1759 a ponder-ous essay in Roman Doric. The road sweeps on to Porthcawl. To avoid such unpleasantness turn right near the village green of Newtown Nottage, its church-tower saddleback rising from the centre of the parapet. Thus you will come to Nottage, where the Tudor court contains tapes-tries of *c.* 1480 from Tewkesbury Abbey and memories of R. D. Black-more, who wrote other novels besides *Lorna Doone*. Blackmore's in-different novel *The Maid of Sker* has for its setting a grim farmhouse isolated in the sand near the coast, nor far from Kenfig.

Leland, King's Antiquary, saw Kenfig just after it had been over-whelmed by a sandstorm in the early sixteenth century. Later inroads of sand reduced the borough still further, but within living memory it had a portreeve, recorder and aldermen, and the ancient charters are pre-served in the village inn, which now serves as guildhall. The church of Maudlam, adjoining the borough, is a rude, kirk-like building with a curious gabled entrance porch set immediately westward of the tower and with an original Celtic cross set upon the roof. There are some fantastic landscapes about Kenfig Pool, a sand-locked lagoon held by pike and conger-eel, and beneath the plover-haunted slough of sand lies the ancient borough of Kenfig.

18   Margam Abbey, Glamorganshire : the Nave

19   Rhossili Church, Glamorganshire

20 The buildings (*c.* 1845) of University College, Swansea

21 Margam Abbey, Glamorganshire : the Orangery, *c.* 1787. Architect unknown

# III

## THE VALE OF NEATH
## SWANSEA BAY    THE GOWER PENINSULA

SINCE we are still in the vicinity of Kenfig there is one excursion that must be made, even though it lies in an area to which industry is quickly giving the *coup de grâce*.   Only the Margam Mountain now preserves the delicious village of Margam, dangerously set on the very margin of industry and coyly hiding itself away from the turmoil of the main road.   Even the oaks of the mountain on its southern face are lopped and stunted, while beyond the railway a mammoth Moloch now building promises tin-strip *ad infinitum*.   But the pleasures of Margam are not technological.

The Cistercian abbey of Margam was founded by Robert, Earl of Gloucester, in 1147, and its thirteenth-century chronicle is preserved at Trinity College, Cambridge.   The slight remains of this abbey stand within the grounds of the mansion erected in 1827, the latter Tudor-Gothic in style with an ambitious central tower and lantern, designed by that Thomas Hopper who worked on the lavish Carlton House in London and whom we shall meet again in Wales.   These ruins, formerly one of the glories of Cistercian architecture, are confined to the magnificent Early-English twelve-sided chapter-house, polygonal as at Abbey Dore (the only two examples of this shape in English Cistercian houses), and its vestibule, while there is a detached vaulted building.   The existing parish church is largely the monastic nave, with an elegant Romanesque façade, gabled, with lancet windows and arcaded side turrets, the whole much restored (18).   Internally the aisles have plaster vaults of the eighteenth century, there are alabaster altar tombs with weepers, and glass by William Morris, while at Sunday matins the choir-boys sit on the *cantoris* side and the choir-girls, in Laudian black diamond hats and gowns with white cravats, looking for all the world like French magistrates, take the *decani* side.

But the grandest feature of Margam has been completely ignored by all topographers old and new.   A few writers, it is true, have glibly announced that part of the monastic site is occupied by "an orangery", but they have omitted to mention that this orangery is one of the finest pieces of post-Reformation architecture in Wales.   Built in 1787 and said to be the largest orangery in the world, it is a joyous festive design in Roman-Doric, with a screen-like sweep of round-headed windows over its rusticated single storey, triglyphs upon the frieze, pedimented wings and a regiment of floral urns upon the cornice (21). With its balustrades and formal terraces, its fountain and exuberant sculpture, it is like a fragment of a *guinguette* or royal pleasance. It is non-Adam in idiom with just a hint of Baroque, and its architect is unknown; one may suspect the hand of Nash, though at this period he was doing nothing but miserable, shoddy work in and about Carmarthen. It is superb, and its setting of giant conifers, laurel trees and Himalayan privet enhances it.

One remembers other things of Margam—the ruined chapel, high on the mountain, which may have been built by the monks for the shepherds living on their *hafod* or summer pasture, the hospitality of the vicarage, with its theological shelves, antiques and Welsh dresser, and the unique collection of Early Christian stones. Of the latter one would single out the sixth-century Bodvic stone, the great Conblein cross of the ninth century and the ornate Enniaun stone. South Wales is rich in such stones, both Roman and sub-Roman (these are more conveniently dealt with under Brecon), and the later enriched crosses of the ninth to twelfth centuries, which are largely Celtic in inspiration and often have Scandinavian characteristics due to Viking inroads. Many of those at Margam and Llantwit have the wheel-head cross which is probably of Manx origin. Their further distribution may be mapped out in Ireland, the Isle of Man, Northumbria and among the Kirkmadrine crosses in the extreme south-west of Scotland.

It is possible to strike northward across the Margam Mountain to the village of Llangynwyd, surmounting a ridge overlooking the valley of the Llynfi. Here, the Welsh Christmas festival of *Mari Lwyd*, or Holy Mary, now quite rare, is still observed with gusto. Its origin is obscure, but it is probably a survival of the medieval plays, identical with the old Christmas play of St. George (as described in Hardy's *Return of the Native*) and the Christmas drama of St. George as performed in Cornwall. The 'Hodening' of Kent is another form of the *Mari Lwyd*. Since we are bound for Neath we may take the mountain road from Llangynwyd, through Maesteg, which is the centre of another coalfield, but which affords good views of the Glamorgan hills dominated by Mynydd Caerau, to Port Talbot, with its acrid smell of copper-works and its floating docks. Here there is a neat Gothic Revival church by J. L. Pearson, whose work may also be seen at Merthyr Tydfil and Treharris, which is characteristic of him and recalls his cathedral at Truro, though here the apse which he elsewhere invariably featured is missing. Beyond is the hamlet of Baglan with its house which Gray the poet knew, its sycamore trees and its single churchyard containing two churches, the modern one having glass by Burne-Jones.

Neath bustles beneath a canopy of smoke at the foot of the Neath river, and beyond fragments of castle and abbey and cobbled church it has few excitements. There is an early nineteenth-century Greek Doric county court, yellow-ochre washed with pale-green quoins, a sober Baptist chapel with Palladian window and portico, and a few buildings of the local blue sandstone. Of the Cistercian abbey of Neath (15), the fairest abbey in Wales according to Leland, with gilded tabernacle-work and tessellated pavements and a roof, according to an earlier writer "like the sky of the Vale of Ebron", there remains nothing but grim twisted fragments, "as black as black", as someone rather unnecessarily pointed out to me. The abbey setting must have been even worse in Borrow's time, for he compared it with "Sabbath in Hell" and associated it with the paintings of the "insane" Jerome Bosch; today there is a sense of continuity in the grim but faintly humorous tag, 'a cemetery without lights' applied to the town by the younger generation, whose *joie de vivre* is, presumably, dampened by magisterial restriction.

Henry Nevinson wrote somewhere that "the right way of entering any country is to slide into it through a river's mouth". I can think of no gloomier approach to South Wales than by making a landfall at Neath, but developing this idea to its logical conclusion and following the river inland is another matter. For the Vale of Neath has yet much beauty, especially on its Brecknock side, for while the Vale proper extends to the village of Pont-nedd-fechan, the extensive watershed of the Neath river ranges well beyond. Leaving the town, the white Cadoxton Lodge where both Stanley the explorer and Sir Oliver Lodge stayed is passed on the left-hand side, and beyond the muddy waterways of Aberdylais is the hamlet of Melyncourt and its waterfalls, formed by the river Clydach. Beyond Resolven, a twisted colliery town snuggling rather uncomfortably between the hills, is the forest of conifers about Rheola, with neglected church set amid rhododendrons and a park of sycamores and oaks hacked in the cause of industrial development. Nearby Maesgwyn House, now a colliery office, is a mildly dramatic house of red brick and stone dressings with gables and bartizan turrets, a house in which Southey as a prospective tenant was interested, though he was frustrated by a cantankerous landlord.

At Glyn Neath one feels the full impact of the spoilation of this lovely valley, even to a race-course. Yet it is an admirable centre for some good mountain excursions into the heart of the *Blaenau*, to the heights of Craig-y-Llyn, the romantic pool of Llyn Fawr and the bright marshlands of Hirwaun. At Aberpergwm, on the other side of the river, is a largely Tudor mansion, gabled, mullioned and towered, a study in brown and grey set against a background of sycamores and silver firs, and nearby is the dower house, Ynyslas House, where Jane Williams entertained bards and harpists and collected the folk-songs of Wales, much as Cecil Sharp did for England.

The intriguing village of Pont-nedd-fechan is set where the hills converge and near the confluence of four mountain streams. This is the Arcadia of these mountains, serene and bright, with its stone bridge over the Neath, its Angel Inn of cream roughcast walls with red-quoined windows and yellow frames, its whitewashed cottages and its grey terrace, in which was born Thomas Stephens, the pharmacist who wrote *The Literature of the Kymry*. There is a story of a haughty Lord Mayor of London who called at the Angel at the beginning of the last century, but was refused refreshment by the equally proud and dogmatic landlady. Nor have all the racy egotists yet gone from this place, for I spoke to a truly Borrovian character who composed verses and who had made love all round the world in the manner of Pierre Loti.

Eastward of the village rises the limestone mass of Craig-y-Dinas, yet another of the legendary resting-places of King Arthur and his knights, from the summit of which one sees the misty coast of Somerset and possibly part of Devon, the Bristol Channel, Mumbles Point, and the copper fumes and lurid glare of the furnaces about Swansea. Below, to the south-west, is the almost inaccessible Sychnant Gorge which divides Glamorgan and Brecknock. In the village the Neath river now branches left and the Melte to the right. Both have bosky glens cutting through the limestone and fretted with caverns and cascades. The majority of these caves and waterfalls are in Brecknock and more conveniently visited from Brecon, since we are here proceeding westward.

Leaving Neath we can barely avoid the oil refineries of Skewen and the vitriol works of Morriston as we round Swansea Bay and enter dockland, where there are rare glimpses, like mental hallucinations, of a ship moored in the cwm between two mountains, for from the road the water is invisible. Swansea, that "horrible and sublime town", as Edward Thomas, the poet, called it, is now, since Hitler's Parthian cavalry of the air blasted the heart out of it, apt to be merely horrible. Yet it has its redeeming features and interest enough if one can forget the cauterised waste (strangely dominated by a derelict mammoth store, with a long sweep of open white arches looking across the rubble like a Moroccan market). A fragment of the fourteenth-century castle is oddly sandwiched between modern offices, the Cross Keys Inn has Georgian casements and is obviously later than 1362, its inscribed date, and the parish church rebuilt by Blomfield is shattered. These now provide the sum of Swansea's earlier buildings, but there are glimpses of a well-mannered late-eighteenth- and early-nineteenth-century town, in Dynevor Place, in terraces along the sea front and in a store in High Street which has segmental-headed windows with urns moulded on the segments. The Royal Institute of 1835 has an Ionic tetrastyle portico and a neat Baptist chapel has a Corinthian portico. This Georgian legacy reminds us of Richard (Beau) Nash, the son of a glass-merchant, who left Swansea to rule the Courts of Pleasure at Bath, and the less-fortunate Richard Savage, who here existed upon a skinflint pension.

Among the amenities of Swansea are the functional Guildhall with minaret-like tower, designed by Sir Percy Thomas and enriched with Brangwyn's panels rejected by the House of Lords, the Glyn Vivian Art Gallery with its Swansea china and Christopher Williams paintings, Singleton Park with a newly created university (20), and a temporary market which displays the mysterious but edible laver-bread and the cockles brought in by the bonneted women of Penclawdd in Gower.

A light railway runs around Swansea Bay—which Savage Landor preferred to the Bay of Naples (of course he saw the former in its pristine excellence)—to Oystermouth, or Mumbles as it is now known, one of the more pleasant resorts on the South Wales littoral. Its substantial castle, crowning a hill overlooking a good anchorage for sailing craft, is mainly thirteenth- and fourteenth-century work, with a perfect gatehouse and a chapel retaining much window tracery. The church has an embattled tower, bells from Santiago and a pillar piscina, and among its many tombstones of mariners is that of Thomas Bowdler who expurgated Shakespeare and Gibbon. Oyster perches are much in evidence on the foreshore, though this industry has declined (in the seventeenth century these oyster-beds were said to be the best in Britain), and off Mumbles Head are two rocky islets, one crowned with the lighthouse of 1794 (8).

We are on the Gower peninsula, on the edge of it but not yet sufficiently removed from the purlieus of Swansea, though at Mumbles the railway ends. Gower has a character of its own, making a compromise between the mountainous *Blaenau* and the fertile *Bro*. It is a barely wooded plateau from which rise several hill-ranges, the highest points being on Cefn Bryn and Rhossili Down, and numerous streams which nowhere reach maturity, but which meander through picturesque glens and miniature ravines. Like parts of Pembroke, this country has a suggestion of an English enclave, its quasi-military churches have a localised *genre* and its villages are feudal compositions.

North-westward from Mumbles is Bishopston, at the head of an attractive, well-wooded limestone glen leading down to the sea. If this is followed to the coast one may strike the red limestone mass of Pwll-du Head, which affords a fine view across Oxwich Bay. About a mile south-west of Bishopston stands the slender embattled tower, top-heavy with two corbel-tables, of Pennard church, and beyond this the combe of the Pennard Pill stream may be followed to the coast, passing the desolate sand-blown castle of Pennard set high above a tidal creek. This is a melancholy relic, late thirteenth century, rectangular with square angle towers, half-filled within with fine detritus and embroidered without with the rare *Draba gizodes*, the Yellow Whitlow Grass, of the Alps.

Returning to the road at Parkmill, both the deep glens which meet here look inviting, but the left-hand, or Green Cwm, will bring one to the chambered cairn at Parc-le-Breos, one of the most perfectly preserved megalithic passage-tombs in Wales. Between Parkmill and Nicholaston, where is a Victorian ornate church in thirteenth-century style containing a hanging pulpit reached by an elaborate groined staircase, the sombre heights of Cefn Bryn dominate the landscape, and on the lower heather-clad slopes is set the modern Penrice Castle.   This is a satisfying house of *c.* 1774, designed by that Anthony Keck who was responsible for some good buildings in and about Worcester.   It has a Roman Doric porch, central pediment and a semi-circular bay to the colourful garden-front. The old castle occupies a rocky bluff and consists of a single irregular bailey strengthened by small circular bastions, gatehouse and two towers on the curtain, mainly thirteenth century, with an unusual keep that is certainly earlier, the whole exhibiting some peculiar characteristics for the specialist.   In the hamlet there is a late Georgian granary raised on stone stilts in the form of toad-stools, with a glass lantern, and, almost opposite, a homely group of farm buildings with a stone *tallat* or barn with open arches.

Penrice church is isolated a mile away, beyond the dingle, and is a humble fane with a Norman moulded chancel arch and, more unusually, a late-medieval entrance arch of oak in the porch.   Oxwich Bay is in sight from this high ground, and the lane drops down to it, passing Sanctuary Farm, glaring white in the noonday sun, with traces of early-sixteenth-century mullions and corbelled-out chimneys, a house probably held by the Knights Hospitallers.   The village of Oxwich, cool and fragrant with cottage-gardens, is set on the verge of the sands in a bay which curves around a fretted coast backed by woodland and heather, and its ancient church of St. Iltyd stands in a grove of trees on a rocky ledge literally overhanging the sea.   The building has fabric ranging over a period between the eleventh and fourteenth centuries, and the font is of such antiquity that it *may* have been brought to an earlier church on this site by St. Iltyd himself, the celebrated disciple of Germanus and master of the learned Gildas.   The tiny chancel of Celtic type has a small, narrow arch, and the wall above this has a neat modern rood against a diapered background.   Above the village are the remains of Oxwich Castle, a fortified manor-house of *c.* 1541 with gatehouse and large round tower embodied in a farmhouse.

It is a good scheme to follow the bed of the Slade stream from Oxwich and then walk around the silted coast, beneath small bastions of limestone, to Port Eynon.   Much of the charm of this place, once a fishing-village, has been dissipated by the caravanserai of week-enders and retired business-men.   The village nucleus retains its whitewashed stone cottages, with inscribed slate panels, around an ancient church which has lost its treasures, before which stands the startling white figure of a lifeboat coxswain petrified on a memorial plinth.   Near the foreshore is the now derelict Salt House, probably of *c.* 1600, which at one time genuinely sheltered pirates (a water-colour of it may be seen in the Art Gallery in Swansea).

The magnificent coast from Port Eynon to Rhossili, excelled only by
the south-western littoral about St. David's, is accessible, and the entire
circuit may safely be made on foot.    Below the golden, lichenous Yellow
Top are the Paviland Caves, in which dwelt Palaeolithic man, and in one
of which was found the celebrated Red Lady of Paviland, no voluptuous
siren this, but the osseous residue, stained red by the action of iron oxide,
of a man of the Cro-Magnon race of the Aurignacian culture.    Beyond
the cliffs of Mewslade Bay the headland plunges into the sea after its
offspring, an outcrop of rock known as Worm's Head with a razor-edged
pinnacle.    The sea surges against this ledge and drowns the causeway
to the mainland.    On the north-west side of these heights ponies whinny
and frisk amid the gorse and bracken.    There is a sheer drop to the table
of sand in Rhossili Bay, and from here Worm's Head looks like a Sphinx.
A more exhilarating spot I have not found, though there must surely be
an element of terror in mid-winter.    It is all perfect: the scudding
Atlantic breaking upon a terrace of glacial drift, the dizzy depths immediately below, the dunes westward, and the red sandstone Rhossili Down
sheltering it in the rear.

In the bleak, grey, windswept village the hoary saddlebacked church
(19) has an interior which comes as a surprise and completes the illusion
that this is Cornwall.    For there are banks of flowers, incense, side-
chapels, rich altar-dressings and pale dancing candle-light of a High
Church order recalling Morwenstow and St. Hilary.    The Protean face
of the bay can be seen from the path which traverses the lower slopes of
the down, above the parterre of arable land and below the bronze autumn
bracken.    I walked this path with a woman who had never been farther
afield than the neighbouring villages of Port Eynon and Llangennydd.
And at the latter village this path arrives by devious ways, passing the red
sandstone height crowned with Sweyne's Houses, early chambered tombs,
of which one is a round tumulus with upright stones and massive capstone.

Llangennydd lies in the hollow south-west of Llanmadoc Hill, its
saddlebacked church-tower rising against the dark Hardings Down.
This church of St. Cennydd, the hermit of Gower, is of peculiar construction, its tower placed north of the nave and its porch on the north, with
Early English fenestration, a square font with scalloped edge, and a generally bare interior accentuated by the absence of aisles.    The adjacent farm
buildings embody some remains of what may have been the *clas* or
Celtic monastery founded by St. Cennydd, which later became a cell of
the Abbey of St. Taurinus at Evreux.    The village of Llanmadoc may be
reached by crossing the hill of that name or by a lane from Kennerstone.
It lies on the edge of the sandy Whitford Burrows and the Llandymor
marshes, on the steep slopes of Llanmadoc Hill with its immense limestone crags.    The church here is Early English, and each of the gables of
its saddlebacked tower has corbie-steps, the only example of this treatment I have encountered in Glamorgan.    There are ancient stones in the

churchyard, and the district is rich in kistvaen, hill-forts and other earth-works.   Nearby Cheriton has a delightfully set church, thirteenth-century, with yet another saddlebacked tower, and not far distant are the scanty remains of Llandymor castle.

A group of inland villages may be taken by a road skirting the Burry valley.   There is Reynoldston, set about a village green on the southern slopes of Cefn Bryn; Knelston, where cows scratch their rumps against the whitewashed walls of a ruined church acting as byre; and Llanddewi, with the last of the five saddlebacked church-towers of Gower.   From Reynoldston the ridge of Cefn Bryn may be crossed by the road that leads into Llanrhidian on the Burry inlet, passing Arthur's Stone, a dolmen celebrated in the ancient Welsh *Triads*.   Overlooking the bright marsh-land north-west of Llanrhidian is ruined Weobley Castle, a medieval fortified manor-house, multi-towered, with thirteenth-century hall and fourteenth-century solar, gatehouse range and chapel.   The coastal road overlooking the Lloughor estuary runs on to Llanmorlais and the drowned wilderness about Penclawdd.

This is cockle-land.   Here the wives of fishermen gather the cockle harvest from the drowned sands by means of short-handled rakes, gathering-sickles and meshed sieves.   Donkeys carry the sacks of cockles from the beds to the foreshore.   The women wear deep-sea boots, flannel dresses, and long-fringed shawls swathed around the neck and over the head, the latter sometimes crowned with a straw bonnet (29).   With these shawls drawn like yashmaks across the faces of the women, the round sieves balanced on their heads and the donkeys heavily laden with pannier-like loads, the scene often recalls a Mongolian pack-train.

This 'costume' of the cockle-women may provide a transition from the Gower dress of the last century.   The *ffedog*, *pais* and *betgwn* (apron, petticoat and bedgown) of the period were often added to by a short jacket and the red 'Gower whittle', a scarf fringed on one side, draped over the shoulders, while the steeple hat was sometimes exchanged for a white bonnet.   But the head-dress was never complete without the white lace head-covering with goffered frills peeping from beneath the hat and hanging down the neck.   The pink-and-blue aprons and linseys had small chequered patterns, the shoulders were often puffed and sometimes a fichu was worn about the shoulders.   Sometimes, too, the 'whittle' was arranged as a head-dress, something like a mantilla, as may be seen in a quite-Spanish engraving, in Lady Llanover's book of Welsh costumes, of a young belle of this remote peninsula balancing an earthenware vessel upon her head.   But we have gone back three or four generations to a more civilised age than this.

Night has fallen over the Lloughor estuary.   There are chevrons of mauve light from the furnaces about Lloughor and Gorseinon.   A tramp-steamer's siren calls out dismally.   Beyond lies the sweet land of Carmarthen.

22 Llanybri Church, Carmarthenshire

23 Cottages near Pont Aber, Carmarthenshire

24   Kidwelly Castle, Carmarthenshire

25   The Village of Pumpsaint, Carmarthenshire

# IV

## CARMARTHEN BAY  THE VALE OF TOWY
## THE COTHI VALLEY

THERE are those who may agree with Baudelaire's dictum that true beauty contains an element of ugliness. Such people will probably have no objection to passing through Llanelly en route for Carmarthen. For the rest of us it is a necessary evil. Yet Llanelly was not always thus, and there were formerly other industries besides tin-plate, steel and anthracite, such gentle pursuits, for example, as spinning and weaving, china, candle-making, wooden ship-building and the manufacture of Welsh steeple hats. While Stepney House remains as a memorial of the slower but more elegant pace of the eighteenth century, an early Georgian building with panelled parapet, enriched modillion cornice and three elaborate rain-water-heads embossed with floral patterns from eaves to ground; internally there is a grand staircase and fluted pilasters supporting a blue and grey enriched cornice.

Much better, then, to hasten to Kidwelly (24) set beside a creek of Carmarthen Bay and still noted for cockles. Kidwelly castle is an imposing, largely intact structure which was begun in the early twelfth century and was one of the two baronial strongholds (Llanstephan was the other) flanking the royal stronghold of Carmarthen, the crucial point in the line of fortresses in the south. It was taken three times and rebuilt after each occasion before Edward I pacified South Wales. Its distinguishing feature is the gatehouse with machicolated gallery between two massive drum-towers, but its most curious features are the large chapel of *c.* 1300 built out from the enceinte towards the river, the huge circular ovens and the conical dungeon, an almost perfect *oubliette*. Technicalities aside, however, this is one of the ideal castles of boyhood; it is *Ivanhoe* and the *Contes Drolatiques*—and the drop-curtain for *Henry the Fifth*. The church is probably in part a remnant of the Benedictine priory founded *c.* 1110, a dependency of Sherborne Abbey. It has a thirteenth-century tower with later broached spire, but is mainly of the following century, cruciform, with long aisleless nave and good piscina and sedilia. Approaching Ferryside the Towy estuary makes a colourful combined sea and landscape, the low-lying range of colour-washed cottages below Llanstephan on the farther shore, the massive square tower of the church above it, the Georgian mansion at a respectable distance, the ruin of a castle drooping over its hill, and, beyond again, the russet, dappled hills.   On these sands the cockle-women (29) work in much the same manner as in Gower, though here carts are used to convey the cockles to the foreshore.   The ferry may, and should, be taken across to Llanstephan, the quiet serene village with its lost, lonely castle overlooking the bay.   This castle was rebuilt *temp.* Henry II and much strengthened and altered in the thirteenth century; it now has outer and inner wards, with a gatehouse on the outer enceinte, which was later adapted as a quasi-keep containing a large hall with some Decorated work. The church in the heart of the village has an embattled tower, hagioscope and Norman font.

Two miles inland over the hill is a village which you may not think worth visiting.   Lovely Llanybri, where live my poet friends Lynette Roberts and Keidrych Rhys, with its whitewashed cottages and solitary fir-tree, its whitewashed church (22), chapel now, with 'four-cornered tower' and slated pyramidal roof and stopped clock, once dedicated to the Blessed Virgin Mary, but alienated by Dissenters in the eighteenth century.   There is the hot sweated breath of the farmyard and the mystical radiance of oil-lamps by night.   And there is—— but Lynette can tell it better than I.

> *If you come my way that is . . .*
> Between now and then, I will offer you
> A fist full of rock cress fresh from the bank,
> The valley tips of garlic red with dew
> Cooler than shallots, a breath you can swank
> In the village when you come.   At noon-day
> I will offer you a choice bowl of cawl
> Served with a 'lover's' spoon and a chopped spray
> Of leaks or savori fach . . .

Another ferry may be taken across the Taf to Laugharne.   This is one of the delightful surprises which Wales holds for the more discerning traveller, a small town which has been the transitory home of such choice spirits as Edward Thomas, Ernest Rhys, Richard Hughes and Dylan Thomas, whilst the beard of Augustus John has frequently graced its strand.   Its architecture is of the sober eighteenth century, and its ample high street is a prosy thoroughfare in which a row of pollarded elms has been lately maimed.   The inn of 1752 has a modest Roman Doric porch, and even the Constabulary has three bow windows.   The miniature Town Hall of 1746, where portreeve and burgesses meet, has Gothic windows and a cream stone belfry tower.   The fishing quarter clusters about the tiny hard of the Corran stream, and boats are moored in the muddy creek.   Crowning the cliff is the ivy-tangled castle embodied in a late-Tudor castellated hall; the gazebo is Georgian.   Turner drew all this one storm-lashed morning.   Sir Guy de Brian, the builder of the

castle, lies in the church at the other end of the town, a cruciform building
with central tower, mainly Early Decorated work, with a niched image
of St. Martin in the porch. The entire place is haunted by more ghosts
than any pisky-plagued Cornish village can claim, and the most ludicrous
and fantastic of all these wraiths, one it would be a real joy to meet, is
surely that of Admiral Laugharne, who appears each St. John's Eve,
naked, ferrying himself across the river in a coracle and bailing it with
a cocked hat.

In the straggling village of St. Clears at the head of the Taf estuary is
a parish church which is a remnant of the only Cluniac monastery in
Wales (though there was another at Malpas in Monmouth), while
Whitland, farther west, has little traces of its celebrated abbey of Alba
Domus, the earliest Cistercian house in Wales, a direct filiation of Clairvaux and always an essentially Welsh monastery in which members of
local leading families took the habit.

The county town is not altogether attractive and is rather unworthy of
its lovely setting, though there is more than a suggestion of earlier
grace and good living, both Georgian and Victorian. Yet the ashes of
history lie smouldering beneath the grey pavements and rough façades
of Carmarthen. Giraldus wrote that the ruined brick walls of a Roman
town were standing in his time. Merlin, that dubious wizard, was here.
The town was burned by Owen Gwynedd in 1137 and the castle was
captured by Owen Glyndowr in 1403. And one of the earliest of recorded *eisteddfodau* was held here in 1451. Of the castle, bits of thirteenth-
century work now peep from behind the late-Georgian façade of a
County Gaol, no longer functional, designed by John Nash to conform to
the humanitarian ethics of Howard, the prison reformer. There are the
slight remains of a Franciscan friary, and the church is largely of the early
fourteenth century. The latter has a wide single aisle, which creates an
effect recalling the twin-naved churches of Denbigh, and a number of
monuments, including the excellent altar-tomb of Sir Rhys ap Thomas,
who struck down Richard III at Bosworth and was knighted by Henry
VII on the field, and the tomb of Major-General Sir William Nott of
Kandahar.

Of the eighteenth-century town there remains the Guildhall, a Palladian mass of 1766 with portico, colonnades and Palladian windows,
and the Ivy Bush Hotel with its old prints and crazy floors and its garden
overlooking the coracle river. Sir Richard Steele of *The Spectator* lived
for some time in another hotel, now demolished, of the same name and
in the same street. There are houses with modillion cornices in Quay
Street and, elsewhere, there is the much-altered Red Lion, Tory head-
quarters in the eighteenth century. The architectural specialist may here
spend some time speculating as to how many of these buildings are the
work of the celebrated John Nash, who spent his early years here and
almost certainly came of local Welsh stock, possibly from Cardigan.

The gaol we know to be his work, as is the monument to that General Sir Thomas Picton who fell leading his brigade at Waterloo. He also designed his own house at Green Gardens and added a moulded plaster ceiling, since removed, to the church; and is locally reputed to have designed the Six Bells Inn and Jeremy's Hotel. All this is so modest as to be nondescript and there is not the slightest inkling of that genius which was to flower; Regent's Park and the Brighton Pavilion were not even in the embryo stage, though the young craftsman, Pugin-like, may well have spent his evenings gently fondling the paper designs of his dreams.

Carmarthen, however, is not a town merely, for it has a country flavour and plays an important part in the lives of the rural communities in the south-west. The Pendre is still the quarter in which countrymen buy their saddles and farming necessities, and in the early-Victorian market there is yet a feast of non-utility goods, bales of flannel and homespuns, *cartheni* or quilting, and the multi-coloured checkered reversible blankets and rugs made of mountain-sheep wool and manufactured on a jacquard loom. Here too is the *Arabian Nights* stall of the rope-maker, spangled and laced and filigreed, and here the cockle-women queen it behind their sacks of shell-fish. It is not so long since women of this area wore silk, satin and cashmere shawls embroidered with floral patterns, gay fichus and those steeple hats which were copied from the head-gear at the Court of James I, as depicted in the portraits by Cornelius Janssens. And the men of this period were like brightly plumed birds, with coats, waistcoats and breeches of coarse blue homespun cloth and stockings of the same colour.

It is autumn in the Vale of Towy and the lanes are strewn with hazel-nuts. The tall pampas grass fidgets in the wind. Silver Towy flows from the heart of the central moorlands, above Ystradffin, through this fabled land of Merlin and out into Carmarthen Bay. You may follow it by road, though it would be better to tramp some of the byways of this lovely vale. At Abergwilli on the northern bank is the palace of the Bishops of St. David's, much modernised, and its ornate chapel dedicated by Bishop Laud lost for ever. Beyond, on the other side of the river, is Llangunnor. Steele lived in the parish and here met his wife, Mary Scurlock, "Dear Pru", though by some freak of fortune it is she and not the essayist who lies in Westminster Abbey. Here too is the grave of Sir Lewis Morris, the Carmarthen-born poet. Near Merlin's Grove is what is said to be the cave in which Merlin was entombed by the resources of the fairy "Lady of the Lake", though Spenser in his *Faery Queen* places the cave at Dynevor, higher up the river. The road crosses the Cothi, descending from the north to meet the Towy, and passes through Llane-gwad to deviate from the river. This is rich pastoral country, placid and not yet dramatic, with slothful Shorthorns beside river banks.

At the Cross Inn I once struck north, passing pink-washed chapel, Victorian church, a cottage with a loose goat frisking in the kitchen and

26  The Towy Valley Carmarthenshire.  On the mound are the ruins of Castle Dryslwyn

27　Carreg Cennen Castle, Carmarthenshire

a farmhouse with a group of nicely thatched haycocks, to Pant glas. The house was disappointing, and there was nothing to link up with the exquisite ruby and clear glass Austrian tankards used here early last century and now in Carmarthen's museum, though the view from this belvedere rewarded me for my pains. The *car llusg*, or wheel-less cart, may sometimes be seen in the hayfields between here and Llanfynydd. Returning to the Towy, the Nelson monument dominates a wooded escarpment on the opposite bank. This is a structure comprising three round towers closely set upon a triangular plan and resembling a pair of binoculars. It was built for Sir William Paxton, a London banker who made a fortune in India, became Mayor of Carmarthen and rebuilt old Middleton Hall. The hall itself is an interesting mansion with the same triangular *motif* as the monument, perhaps inspired by Sir Thomas Tresham's triangular lodge, an Elizabethan curiosity at Rushton in Northamptonshire. The architect, C. R. Cockerell, was the friend and collaborator of Nash, and it was not typical of him (in spite of his Hindoo effort at Seizincote in Gloucestershire) to undertake such Beckfordesque whimsy, though the ample coffers of Sir William probably played a persuasive role.

On the road to Llangathen the shattered hill-top ruins of Drysllwyn castle dominate the landscape. This was obviously a sort of blockhouse designed to prevent any assault from the south from penetrating up-river. Like the neighbouring castles of Carreg Cennen and Dynevor, it was generally in Welsh hands, though it ended, inevitably, with the English. The village of Llangathen is set in a little Arcady of woodland, hill and water beneath the Grongar Hill of John Dyer, poet and painter *manqué*. Dyer, son of a local solicitor, was born in the parish and lived at Aberglasney House. He studied art in Italy, caught malaria and returned home to enter the Established Church. His poems, *The Golden Fleece*, *Grongar Hill* and others, had a transient vogue, but his immortality is largely due to an Ode by Wordsworth being addressed to him, much as the Old Man of Ross was made immortal by Pope. Aberglasney is a neat Georgian house with Ionic portico, and there are the remains of an earlier gatehouse and a curious rude quasi-cloister. The church, partly thirteenth-century, has an embattled corbelled tower, Perpendicular clerestory, Tudor enriched communion table and the effigied tomb of Bishop Rudd, portrayed in the ruffed collar and leg-of-mutton sleeves of the non-liturgical early-Stuart dress.

Beyond Llangathen the Towy may be crossed by a bridge which affords striking views of the valley and the series of miniature tablelands sloping down to the river. Southward is Llandebie, a place with some surprising links with the past. There is a tradition that the Glynhir factory near here exported arms to France during the Revolution, and that the proprietors, the Huguenot du Buisson family, were the first people in Britain to hear of the victory at Waterloo.

You need travel no farther than Llanfihangel Aberbythych, however, to see Golden Grove, where that eminent divine Jeremy Taylor took refuge with the Earl of Carberry during the Civil War. Taylor, the son of a Cambridge barber, became a favourite of Archibshop Laud, chaplain to Charles I, and a fellow of All Souls at Oxford, so that naturally enough he threw in his lot with the Royalists, and when their cause was lost he came to Golden Grove. Here, to quote his own words, "In the great storm which dashed the vessel of the Church all in pieces I was cast on the coast of Wales; and in a little boat thought to have enjoyed that rest and quietness which in England, in a far greater, I could not hope for." Here he wrote *Golden Grove, Holy Living* and *Holy Dying*, the latter inspired by the griefs of both himself and his patron, for he had lost his three sons almost at a stroke and the earl had lost his wife. But that Elizabethan house, the same in which the young Nash had later designed a bathroom, is no more. There is nothing here of the pious bishop; rather is it the personality of the pompous Sir Jeffrey Wyattville that is extruded from these walls, for this pastiche was designed by him. It has corbie-stepped gables, a massive saddlebacked tower and mullioned fenestration. When I was there the place was derelict, the drive mossy and carpeted with bronze autumn leaves, the regimental line of clipped yews guarding the terrace no longer suave and spruce, though a solitary rose bloomed in the wilderness. The park is well-wooded, though it is not the enchantment that its name would imply, and the duck-shooting in this area is said to be the best in the county.

Just before Llandilo the heights of Dynevor Park, massed with oaks and Spanish chestnuts, seem to rise sheer from a lawn. The approach to the town from this direction, the steep hill of terraced houses leaping the bridged river, looks promising. Once in the town, however, and much of this charm is dissipated; the church was completely cobbled by Sir Gilbert Scott and there is a spate of new buildings. Happily, Dynevor Park, with the broken towers of its castle, is accessible. Dynevor was one of the three regal palaces of Wales and its possession was always keenly contested by the wrangling kinsmen of the house of Rhys ap Gruffydd. The last of the family to hold it was Rhys ap Rhys, who was compelled to surrender it to King Edward. This led to the great South Welsh insurrection of 1287, when Rhys ap Maredud seized Dynevor in a day, but when the Earl of Cornwall's forces prepared an assault the Welsh garrison made a midnight sortie and escaped to the hills. The new Dynevor Castle is a striking effort of 1856, rectangular, with machicolated walls, square corner towers capped with candle-extinguisher turrets, and an arcaded porch, and it is set in almost-lyrical woodland and pasture where white kine graze.

The excursion *par excellence* in this area is that to Carreg Cennen, an eagle's nest towering upon a precipitous rock above the Cennen stream near the hamlet of Trapp. This is the last of the three great castles of the area, the last refuge of the native Welsh princes when Drysllwyn and Dynevor had fallen. It was a castle built by desperate men in desperate straits, and its sheer natural walls of limestone were sufficient guarantee of its impregnability. Starvation only could have reduced it, and when Glyndowr subdued the rest of Carmarthenshire in 1403 the English castellan held out through more than a year's blockading—the end of this issue is unrecorded. Yet such were the resources of both sides that it changed hands four times in a decade. Later it became the haunt of outlaws, for which, with its subterranean tunnel channelled through the rock, it was eminently suited. We disagree for once with the pedantic archaeologist who says that Carreg Cennen is of the thirteenth century. For there is about it an air of timelessness, as though it belonged to no age but were rather a figment of the imagination, an air of Romanticism (eighteenth-century engravers almost queued up to draw it), a flavour which faintly recalls Castillon, and its reputed foundation by Urien, a knight of Arthur's Round Table, does but pile romance on romance.

Outside the small town of Llangadock is the mansion of Abermarlais, rebuilt early last century for that Admiral Foley who had led the fleet into action at the Battle of the Nile. The halcyon days of this domain, however, were those of an earlier house, when its owner was the wily, martial Gruffydd ap Nicholas who supported the Duke of York. Abermarlais was then a veritable hornet's nest of intrigue, with the family splitting over York and Lancaster. Almost the last of this family to hold the estate was that Sir Rhys ap Thomas already alluded to, a knight of fine fettle who died clothed in the Franciscan habit. The English Wars of the Roses had no small influence upon Welsh policy and history, though the Welshmen were divided (when were they not?)—in general the west supporting the Lancastrian cause and the east the Yorkist, and at Mortimer's Cross in 1461, where Owen Tudor fell, Welsh fought Welsh. With the death of Prince Edward at Tewkesbury, Henry Tudor became the heir and representative of the House of Lancaster. The Welsh were quick to realise the opportunity afforded by a Welshman on the English throne and they submerged their differences, uniting and rallying about the Lancastrian standard. Henry VII was loyal to his pledges and he reversed the anti-Welsh policy in vogue up to that time and appointed Welshmen as sheriffs for Welsh counties, though he realised that the only solution of the Welsh problem lay in stripping Wales of her individuality and tradition and merging it with England. Thus it is from this period that Welsh stability and prosperity began, as it is from this period that Wales began to lose everything she cherished.

The Carmarthen Van, which now appears eastward, may be taken from either Llangadock or Llandovery. Either route is rough and well-nigh impracticable for motorists, though it may with difficulty be taken as far as Llanddeusant, the last village facing the formidable chocolate-coloured cliffs. From Llangadock you will follow the quiet valley of the Sawdde until you turn north-eastward to the mountain village, with its solitary inn and church. East and south-east runs the long ridge of the Brecknock Beacons, from which the Carmarthen Van is separated by a deep cleft, though the higher of the two Vans is actually in Brecknock. It is a sombre and tortuous landscape with a warm fantasy, best seen in the last reddening light after sunset, as James Dickson Innes, the Llanelly-born painter who died of tuberculosis at the age of twenty-seven in 1914, has framed it. There is all the unexpected thrill of the Grand Canyon in the deep, buzzard-haunted corries of this range, which the late Thoresby Jones described as "one of Nature's more obvious contributions to Cubist art".

Beneath the north precipices are the stone-locked lakes of Llyn y Fan Fawr, the source of the Tawe, and Llyn y Fan Fach. The latter is rich in those lake legends which abound in the medieval folk-tales of Wales, once told by the *cyfarwyddiaid*, or professional story-tellers, and later collected together in the *Mabinogion*. Briefly, this story is of the wooing by a local peasant of a fey maiden who lived in the lake and who, upon their betrothal, brings forth her aqueous dowry in the shape of many cattle. Three sons were born to them, who afterwards became the celebrated physicians of Myddfai. Many years passed and the husband, forgetting his wife's early vow that she would leave him if he struck her three blows, prodded, tapped or otherwise gently laid his hands upon her in rebuke for some trivial misdemeanour, and on the third occasion the callous little minx picked up her traps and solemnly walked back into the lake, taking with her everything she had brought out, even to the four oxen ploughing in the fields, which followed her and dragged the plough below the water.

From Llanddeusant another rough road may be taken to Llandovery, passing the remote Talsarn chapel and entering the grey village of Myddfai, where the physicians born of the watery maiden practised their magical arts. Llandovery, situated near the confluence of the Bran and Gwydderig, is thoroughly Welsh in essence and has so far resisted those 'civilised' veneers which have changed the face of Llandilo. Its market-place is yet cobbled, and at frequent horse-fairs as many as five hundred horses are tethered in the main street. Its cattle-market is reputed to be the second in Wales, and it takes two whole days a month to dispose of sheep alone, between four and five thousand being sold in a single day. Its houses are largely early nineteenth century, often embodying earlier fabric, and there is hardly a window but has an architrave about it. The Town Hall, with belfry tower and arched treatment, is of the same period, and the inns, the Bear, the King's Head and the Red Lion, are honest-to-goodness Borrovian pubs where the chromium-plate has not encroached. They have homely facades, these inns, with penthouse additions or minia-ture colonnades, and the sire of them all is Borrow's own hostelry, the Castle. Here there are beds of two kinds, soporific beds for a clientele largely composed of farmers and parents of the boys at the college, and

28    Sheep Shearing at Dyffryn Mymbyr, Carnarvonshire

29    Cockle Gatherers at work in the Towy Estuary, Carmarthenshire

30　The Elan Forest in the Upper Towy Valley, Cardiganshire

beds which are museum-pieces, for one is the four-poster in which
Borrow slept and another is a half-tester in which Nelson is reputed to
have lain on his way to Carmarthen (or was it Milford and Lady Hamilton?). This hotel is filled with faded photographs of Llandovery School
Rugby fifteens and cricket elevens, generations which have seen dire
changes. The only other public school in Wales is Christ's College at
Brecon, and when the two rival schools meet there is a glorified bun-fight.
The college itself, neo-Gothic, was founded in 1846 by a local haberdasher
who had made a fortune in London, and above the entrance is the
inscription (in Welsh) *Better Learning than Gold*, as perhaps the good
draper had realised too late.

Of Llandovery's antiquities there remain but the decayed fragment of
a castle of *c.* 1100 with an oval motte and two parish churches, one, with
fifteenth-century tower and low-side window, at Llandingat and the
other, of much the same date but embodying some bricks of a Roman
station, at Llanfair-ar-y-Bryn. Rhys Pritchard was vicar of the former
church. Pritchard was a friend of Laud, became vicar of his native town
and Chancellor of St. David's, was cured of liquor by the sight of a
ludicrous drunken goat, henceforward had Puritan leanings and wrote
the celebrated *Canwyll y Cymry* or *The Welshman's Candle*, which, like
Keble's *Christian Year*, has gems among the dross. The townspeople of
Llandovery are re-discovering Borrow's *Wild Wales*, but I doubt whether
there are half-a-dozen copies of Pritchard's masterpiece in the town.
This area has also been remarkable for its evangelicals of a certain formidable caste, the last of which was the Victorian Timothy Richard,
alias Li-Ti-mo-lai, one of the builders of modern China.

The head of the Towy (30) can be reached via the purlieus of Ystradffin,
passing the goggle-eyed bridge of Dolauhirion and skirting the green
Cilicwn Forest to lovely Cilicwm and Rhandyrmwyn. Cross the bridge
near the pyramidal hill called Dinas and walk along the Towy banks,
pranked with larch and ash and glistening bracken, in search of rare
marsh-plants, the asphodel and the butterwort, locally known as 'cuckoo's
slipper'. The uplands about here are naked and wild, treeless and
treacherous with loose shale. Near the solitary chapel and farm of
Ystradffin, under the lee of Dinas, is the elusive narrow entrance to Twm
Shon Catti's cave. Twm was the seventeenth-century thief-hero of these
hills, a low rascal with a keen sense of humour that got him an heiress
to wife and a comfortable sinecure as sheriff of the county, but you can
read the prolix Borrow on this theme. There are some hill walks in this
area which are well worth doing if you like being quite alone in a wilderness of moorland, bog and scree, particularly towards the head of the
valley, where one strikes the old drovers' track from Abergwesyn to
Tregaron. The area is referred to on p. 54.

It is possible to follow the sinuous Cothi to Pumpsaint by a road which
wheels westward from below Dinas, but you may prefer to return to

Llandovery and take the scenic Lampeter road from Llanrhwda, passing through the glen of the Dulais and then climbing over the Bwlch Cefn Sarn pass. But any pretext is welcome which takes you into Caio, slightly north-east, with its massive grey church, the Roman square tunnels and later workings of the abandoned gold-mines, and Dolaucothy, the eighteenth-century seat of the Johnes family and the house which shook Borrow out of his usual self-sufficiency and moved him to envy. From Pumpsaint (25), where five saints were reputedly born at a birth, the Welsh quintuplets of the middle ages, either bank of the Cothi leads to Llansawel, charmingly set on the little Marlais. Here the church contains hagioscopes, three low-side windows and a font attached unusually to the western wall. The way from here to Talley passes Edwinsford, a small mansion of early-seventeenth-century date containing enriched plaster ceilings, and re-crosses the Cothi. The scanty ruins of Talley Abbey stand below the twin lakes in the valley of the Afon Dulas. Founded for Premonstratensians by Rhys ap Gruffydd in the twelfth century, it was a filiation of St. John's in Amiens and the only monastery of this order in Wales. There has been much confusion over the origin of this house, but, contrary to some opinions, it is certain that it was Premonstratensian from the beginning. The architectural affinities between the conventual church here and that at Strata Florida are explained by principles common to both White Canons and Cistercian monks, both, for example, having the transeptal eastern chapels.

Re-cross the Cothi to Abergorlech, where is a farm of the native 'longhouse' type, and where the red flannel such as scared the French invaders was made at an old pandy dismantled a decade ago. Follow the river to Brechfa, the haunt of poker-faced contemplative anglers, for the Cothi is rich in salmon and trout. The return to Carmarthen may be made via the chess-board country of Llanllawdog and Llanpumpsaint.

And here it must be recorded that there is within this area a truly Welsh inn that is a delight. Its interior has Welsh dressers, china dogs, glistening brass, roaring fire and flickering light of oil-lamps. There is no bar, only a settle disposed about the fireside. Shepherds quaff their *cwrw da* and there is here no lingua franca, nothing but the soft, pure Welsh. And, since some of the things that are Caesar's must be held *for* Caesar, I will not reveal its name.

31  Tenby, Pembrokeshire.  The Gascoyne Rock on the North Sands

32 Tenby, Pembrokeshire. The Harbour

# V

## TENBY AND CALDEY ISLAND    MILFORD HAVEN.    ST. BRIDE'S BAY    DEWISLAND

I OFFER no apology for beginning this area from Tenby (32), most pleasant of all resorts on the Welsh littoral and one which, in truth, attracts fewer aesthetic morons than do its northern competitors. The Victorians found it enchanting, and the Gosses have painted it in glowing colours. Ralph Henry Gosse's *Tenby: A Seaside Holiday*, published in 1856, is a key to a magical land of anemones and amphibious ballets, and Sir Edmund's later *tour-de-force*, *Father and Son*, hints at the schoolboy wonder of this place. Indeed, the view of the harbour from the terraced cliffs is so toy-like that it must be the child's ideal playground, for what other harbour filled with small craft has a hill-castle overlooking it? (Only Gorey in Jersey can be compared with it.) And though the Brixham smacks are now rarely seen and the priest goes no longer from St. Julian's chapel to bless the fishing fleet, as he yet does at Concarneau in Brittany, the harbour still pulsates with life.

Near the quay are the baths erected for Sir William Paxton in 1806, and above an entrance here is a Greek quotation from Euripides. Much of the town is of this period, and in an evening's walk along St. Julian's Street the eye catches filigreed Georgian fanlights lighted from within. Those were the halcyon days of Tenby, the Tenby of Charles Norris's etchings, published about 1812, a year of augury. The harbour was filled with luggers and trawlers unloading oysters and sole. Pretty prawn-sellers walked the streets. The sedan-chair was here used as late as 1872. There are much older relics, however, dating from a period of Tudor prosperity when Flemish weavers were established here. The castle is a thirteenth-century fragment with small, round keep, entrance gateway, and projecting bastion looking out to the fortified islet of St. Catherine, patron saint of spinners. The inner town retains a substantial section of the town wall of *c.* 1458, a fortified curtain strengthened by bastions and having one remaining gate protected by a peculiar semi-circular barbican. In a narrow alley is the Tudor Merchant's House of *c.* 1500, its projecting mullioned windows having arched heads. The parish church is largely of Perpendicular style and is somewhat remarkable for its raised choir over a long flight of steps. It contains, *inter alia*, a fifteenth-century barrel-vaulted roof with carved figure-head corbels, seventeenth-century carved oak pulpit, elaborate alabaster tombs of merchants with their heads resting upon peacocks, and a doorway with a curious ogee head enriched with the four-leaved rose-flower.

The low-lying island a few miles off-shore is Caldey, the island of Ynys y Pyr. It is a self-contained manor of which the Cistercian Abbot of Chimay in Belgium is lord, the prior of the Caldey monastery being his representative, and the old seigneurial laws are still maintained. Caldey is thus a kind of *imperium in imperio*. Perhaps the crossing is best made by the island boat navigated by a lay-brother. Beyond the tiny quay and the brow of the hill with its calvary is a landscape which has a Mediterranean flavour, the red-tiled whitewashed villas clustered about a monastery of white roughcast walls and red-tiled roofs broken up by towers and turrets and Romanesque windows, an Edwardian fantasy. Certainly it is dramatic. There may be in it a suggestion of Hollywood and one's local Odeon, but at least it is original and exciting, and if one must tie it down to some particular milieu it is probably that of Lombardy. Yet there is little of the theatre, indeed none, in the Cistercian life which goes on, *mutatis mutandis*, as it did at Margam, Strata Florida and Valle Crucis before the Reformation. The Spartan rule of *laborare est orare*, work is prayer, remains, and in the early morning the prior will be found at the head of his flock working in the fields.

In the hamlet is the lily-pond with its balconied bridge, the village *rialto* on which the gossips meet. Here, too, the *familiars*, or workers employed by the monastery, angle for carp. Beyond rock-garden and shrine is the village church of St. David, with screened chancel and Oberammergau wood-carvings. Roses blush in the pergolas of the terraced gardens, and in Anglican days (at the monastery's foundation in 1906 *et seq.*) peacocks strutted here. (The last monastery at which I saw peacocks was Tongerloo in the Belgian Campine.) Beyond the monastic gatehouse strangers are normally forbidden to go, but I recall the cream-walled cloisters, the oak-panelled refectory with open timber roof, the octagonal kitchen inspired by the Abbot's Kitchen at Glastonbury, and the abbatial house. The latter, with its minaret-like tower, is pre-Reformation in majesty of conception, with an unusual private chapel exhibiting marked Italian influence and containing a marble pavement and an altar of pink alabaster.

South-westward is the original priory of the Tironesian reform, with fortified gatehouse, church, refectory and prior's house grouped about a cobbled court. These rude buildings of twelfth- and thirteenth-century date represent one of the early cradles of Celtic Christianity, for they are the successors to the seventh-century *clas* founded by St. Samson. St. Iltyd was here and St. Gildas and St. Dubricius (Tennyson's 'Dubric the High Saint') and SS. David, Malo and Paul of Leon. This early monastery became a great school of learning on the model of Lerins—

another monastic island resembling Caldey. Nothing could be more eloquent than this hoary church, with its crooked stump of a tower, its cobbled floor and archaic barrel-vaulting, its Ogham stone and its sanctuary-lamp yet lighted by the presbyter's assistant. Yet though the monastic life dominates Caldey, there is the music of the sea as well as of Gregorian plainchant. There are blood-splashed hedges of fuchsia. Golden gorse blooms for ever. The cliff-tops are mantled with gilded samphire, purple orchids and pink thrift like coral. Goldfinches and bullfinches dart about poplars, pines and rhododendrons. Above the grape-coloured sea wheel the oyster-catchers and an occasional puffin with brilliantly coloured, parrot-like beak.

This island fever cannot last and we must return to the villas of Tenby, piled high on the mainland. At Begelly we may yet see some of the gypsies of Augustus John's early paintings (the painter himself was born in Tenby), and beyond the great marsh with its summer yellow irises at the back of the town, there is the road to Gumfreston, St. Florence and Lamphey, all village Arcadies with ecclesiological excitements, the last having the ruins of an episcopal palace (36), the country home of medieval prelates. An exploration of the coast is best made from Penally on the eastern slope of the ancient Ridgeway, and in the churchyard here are two ancient crosses, one enriched with mouldings of Northumbrian inspiration and the other with perfect wheel-head enriched with plait-work. Most of these south Pembroke churches conform to a localised type, featuring quasi-military towers and hagioscopes on either side of the chancel arch, sometimes in the shape of wide alcoves and sometimes cut right through like passages, as at Bosherston, Stacpole, Johnston, Uzmaston, Castlemartin, St. Florence, Marloes and here at Penally.

In this deeply fretted coast, alternating between limestone and red sandstone, are the Lydstep caves, accessible only at very low water, and beyond Shrinkle Haven, where is another change in the geological formation, is Manorbier. This village is charmingly set about a combe, and Giraldus Cambrensis held it to be the sweetest spot in all Wales. Of course he was biased, for he was born there, though in our own time Augustus John would seem to support him in this view. Gerald de Barri was a militant ecclesiastic who had some affinities with Peter Abélard; he was a scholar and the author of some fifteen books, of which the most popular are the *Itinerary through Wales* and the *Autobiography*; he was shrewd, witty, ambitious, eloquent and a virulent critic, and although he loved Wales above all, his pen frequently scourged his countrymen (indeed, the *Itinerary* contains a paradoxical catalogue of Welsh virtues and vices). He loved the Paris of St. Louis and was frequently in Rome; he was a favourite at court, retired in his old age to Lincoln and died at St. David's. But Manorbier remained the darling of his heart. The castle (34) was probably founded by Gerald's grandfather, John de Barri, but the earliest fabric is contemporary with Gerald himself and is probably

the work of his brothers.    What remains is a remarkable example of a
Norman baron's estate complete with all its appendages, church, mill,
dovecote and pond.    It has a single ward, no keep, but a strong projecting
gatehouse and a drum-tower.    Internally, the buildings are of two
periods, *temp.* Henry II and the early years of Edward I, and include
chapel and hall on barrel-vaulted undercroft.    The parish church is a
composite structure with early barrel-vaults, a curious extension of the
rood-loft in the north aisle and the thirteenth-century recumbent effigy
of a de Barri.

The cliffs of Manorbier Bay can be tramped as far as Stacpole, the next
coastal village.    Motorists have to proceed via Lamphey, a welcome
pretext to see Hodgeston church, with its beautiful Decorated chancel
studded with ball-flower and containing double piscina and triple sedilia.
Stacpole Court, a plain stone mansion of *c.* 1735 with an earlier groined
and vaulted undercroft, stands at the head of a long creek transformed into
a lake rich in water-lilies, and Cheriton church has good monuments and
hagioscopes.    The coast beyond Bosherston must be explored on foot.
Just west of St. Govan's Head is the intriguing chapel of St. Govan,
tightly wedged into a cleft of the limestone bastions, a thirteenth-century
oratory, gabled and bell-coted, with stone fittings and an adjoining rock-
hewn cell (35).    Tradition identifies Govan with the Arthurian Gawain,
but a dedication to Cofen, wife of an early Welsh king, seems more
plausible, though Baring-Gould supplies another alternative and cites
the Irish St. Gobhan.    The rock scenery in this area is fantastic and,
ranging from St. Govan's to the Stack Rocks, includes in consecutive
order the Huntsman's Leap, a fissure in the cliff once leapt by a horseman
who immediately afterwards died of retrospective terror; Bullslaughter
Bay, with its twisted strata; the Sunken Forest; the Devil's Punch Bowl,
an immense cauldron with sheer rock sides; and, finally, the Stacks (41),
isolated masses of limestone haunted by cormorants, puffins, razorbills
and guillemots.

From Bosherston a network of lanes, in autumn piled high with
mangels, connects a few scattered parishes containing the lonely churches
of St. Petrox, St. Twynnel's and Warren, all of local type, two containing
hagioscopes and the last crowned with one of the rare spires of Pembrokeshire.    The gatehouse of Orielton stands out against a dark wood.    This
is probably the modern successor to the house described by Giraldus as
haunted by 'unclean spirits'.    A few years ago the tenant of Orielton
was a Spanish count, a direct descendant of the Royal line of Navarre,
one of whose ancestors was Grand Chamberlain to the Emperor Maxi-
milian of Mexico, and whose family included that St. Veremundo whose
shrine is at Arellano in Italy.    Such are some of the strange memories
that linger in this remote and beautiful province.    Yet it is an area in
great part no longer either remote or beautiful, for the Admiralty, War
Department and Air Ministry in one combined operation have done their

33   The Palace of St. David's, Pembrokeshire

*From Paul Sandby's "Views in . . . Wales" (1775)*

34   Manorbier Castle, Pembrokeshire

*From a print by St. Richard Hoare (c. 1800)*

36  Lamphey Palace, Pembrokeshire : ruins of the

35  St. Govan's Chapel, Pembrokeshire

damnedest to destroy it. The population of Castlemartin parish has dropped to half since the beginning of the late war. From St. Govan's Head to Castlemartin the land is littered with derelict, ruined camps and some score of abandoned farmsteads. No doubt these ruins will remain until future helicopter-flying generations schedule them as ancient monuments. The abandoned medieval chapel of Flimston, its belfry damaged by gun-fire, is also in this area.

There is little hint of this desolation in Castlemartin itself, a village notable for giving its name to the black, long-horned cattle. Here are a perfect old circular pound of stone and a church delightfully set in a wooded dell, the latter of unusual construction and recalling that of Manorbier. Nearby is a fragment of what appears to have been an ancient rectory, comprising two small arcades and a shaft with capital carved with crude faces. In the picturesque churchyard lie many mariners shipwrecked off Linney Head. To the north-west is a broad valley thinly screened by wind-blown trees, and to the south is the splendid Freshwater Bay backed by sand-dunes. Surf-riding is possible here though there is a dangerous backwash. Near the western end is the Irish-looking colony of gabled driftwood huts thatched with rushes. In these is stored the laver weed which is made into laver-bread, the Irish sloak. When in sufficient quantity it is boiled and compressed into cakes and sent to market. Cooked and seasoned and resembling spinach with a dash of iodine, it is esteemed as a breakfast dish. And so one comes to Angle, the last village of this peninsula, of which a former squire, John Mirehouse, was a school-fellow and friend of Byron.

I came to Angle on a winter's night and fell in love with it. The long rows of colour-washed cottages, a stream or open culvert on either side, and the embattled inn jettied over a colonnade and containing gay painted cast-iron staircase and an ivory model of a Chinese house-boat. The inn was built by a speculating colonel on his return from the Boer War, for he thought the railway would come. The railway came—but only so far as Pembroke. I woke to find rain glistening on gull-perched roofs, gardens blushing with pink flowers and bells ringing from the church-tower silhouetted against the silver Haven. Angle has a queer collection of antiquities oddly jumbled together. The church is severely restored, and contains little but an unusual sedilia, but in its churchyard is the detached chapel of St. Anthony, built in 1447 and used as a seamen's chapel, a small gabled oratory, containing piscina and the effigy of a priest. Opposite are a peel-tower and a circular dovecote, while on the nearby cliff is one of Henry VIII's blockhouses, designed to guard the entrance to the Haven but never completed. The village street runs on to a small disused quay beneath a rocky headland. Here the beauty of the immense fiord of Milford Haven is revealed, the distant shores rising into gentle hills. The fort on Thorne Island—all these forts are later variants of the Martello tower—has been converted into a hotel, a strange ivory tower for those who are able to resign themselves to being as isolated as lighthouse-keepers, penned in the garrison chambers grouped about the courtyard. Yet it is a spot nicely calculated to inspire romance, and the heiress who opened the hotel married her boatman. It is possible to hire a boatman to take you over to Dale, but the upper reaches of Milford Haven cannot be ignored.

Pembroke, on a pill or creek of the Haven, has a gloomy single street with nothing of interest beyond the castle. Yet this is a castle, standing upon its rock and almost sea-girt when the tide is in, which gives the town character enough. Where Caerphilly squats and broods, Pembroke seems to be alert, even rampant. We have already noted that T. E. Lawrence grouped Pembroke with Caerphilly and Fougères, and that should be sufficient indication of its merits. Originally built by Arnolf de Montgomery in 1090, it became the chief seat of the Earls Palatinate of Pembroke and here was born Henry Tudor, later Henry VII. The gatehouse is of unusual design, having an external barbican placed obliquely and a curious embattled flying-arch connecting two round towers on the inner side. But the grand feature of Pembroke is the massive cylindrical donjon, the finest in Wales, as Coucy, the first military tower in Europe, is on the Continent, though here there are the added rarities of a stone dome and a postern on the second floor. The latter is a precaution rarely found in round keeps, which normally had only one entrance—or exit, even at Château Gaillard. The town's two churches are of little interest, but at Monkton over the bridge is the church of a Benedictine priory founded in 1098, with barrel-vaulted nave and a rare chamber over the south porch.

Taking the east bank of the Cleddau you will pass through Upton, with its perfect thirteenth-century castle gatehouse fronting a modern mansion, to Carew. Here is yet another major castle, rectangular, with a three-quarter drum at each angle (38). Its early history is closely linked with Nesta, that highly born, highly active, prolific little trollop, and its later history with that Sir Rhys ap Thomas, who built the Tudor west front, rich in mullioned fenestration and armorial work, and who here gave a tournament and fete which hit the society headlines of the time and is minutely described in the Cambrian Register. Carew for a small place has wealth. Its church preserves most of its original features and tombs of the Carews, there is a detached chantry chapel, a fifteenth-century fortified rectory and a perfect wheel-head cross, probably ninth-century, elaborately carved. Beyond the old bridge of Canaston, where is a striking composition made up of bridge, church and weir, is Llawhaden with a ruined episcopal palace of St. David's, strongly fortified and overlooking the wooded valley of the Eastern Cleddau. The road to Haverfordwest winds through pastoral country, the Prescelly Mountains now rising to the north-west, and skirts Slebech Park, containing the ruins of a Knights Templar's church, and Picton Castle. The latter was

37 The Village of Solva, near St. David's, Pembrokeshire

38 Carew Castle, Pembrokeshire. The Tudor North Front

39  The Harbour, Milford Haven, Pembrokeshire

altered about 1740 and received some neo-Norman additions early last century, so that it is now a composite mansion recalling Chirk.

Taking the west bank of the Cleddau, one crosses the Haven by the ferry from Neyland. This section of the fiord is sullied by industry, but there is contrast and movement in naval activity and Sunderland flying-boats. At Rosemarket is the dovecote of the demolished great house and a gabled church of Welsh type, and at Llangwm farther up-river the wives of the fishermen until quite recently did the job their menfolk should have done, gathering cockles and oysters and carrying their creels as far afield as Tenby. Or you may take Haverfordwest by way of Milford (39), where Lady Hamilton lived in the forlorn Italianate mansion in sub-tropical grounds sloping down to the shores of a tidal creek. In the eighteenth century Milford took part in the whaling industry, an enterprise stimulated by the introduction of some Quaker families from Nantucket in America, the home of expert whalemen. Many of these Quakers remained and died here, as the Welsh had founded Quaker colonies in Pennsylvania in the previous century.

Haverfordwest, towered and turreted and set upon a hill above the Cleddau, is not merely a county town, for it is the capital of that province whose sobriquet is Little England beyond Wales. Its inhabitants are descendants of Flemings, Normans, Norsemen and English, their language often a dialect compounded of words borrowed from these tongues. It stands on the edge of the line dividing the 'Welshery' from the southern English enclave, a division roughly marked by the line of Norman castles. Architectural characteristics have been noted, and there is further evidence of this ethnological distribution in the Scandinavian place-names about Milford Haven, while the comparative sparsity of dissenting chapels in the south is also eloquent. The town has charm and dignity, which are largely derived from the Georgian houses and the terraced height above the castle. The latter is mainly thirteenth-century work, rectangular, with massive round towers and a square bastion projecting on the east; both Henry II and Richard II were there, and in 1405 it withstood a siege by Glyndowr and his French allies. The Castle Hotel huddles beneath the monster which gives it its name, a Georgian house of which the cellar contains the blocked four-centred arched fireplace, c. 1490, of an earlier building. Nor is this the only architectural palimpsest, for two Elizabethan enriched fireplaces remain in the later building occupied by a bookshop. Almshouse and grammar school have been rebuilt, but the purlieus of the parish church have an air. Here are neat Victorian terrace-ranges, neo-Gothic, with all the doors and windows in square hood-moulds, the Mariner's Inn with Ionic porch, and the old Butter Market with groined vault over open-pillared arcades. There are three churches, St. Thomas's, rebuilt but retaining a late fifteenth-century tower, St. Martin's, towered and spired, with trefoiled piscina, and St. Mary's. The last is one of the greater parish churches of Wales and is rich in Early

English work, especially in the carved capitals of the arcades, where are women in head-dresses, an ape playing a harp and a pig playing a *crwth* or old Welsh violin, these last probably designed as sly digs at the Welsh. The lacunared oak roof is contemporary with the more celebrated roof of St. David's Cathedral, and among the monuments is the effigy of a pilgrim wearing the sclavine or pilgrim's robe, the scrip adorned with the scallop-shells of Santiago da Compostella.

At Poyston near the town is the Georgian mansion in which General Sir Thomas Picton was born. Poyston belongs to an age when the local gentry held an annual Little Season in the town, when the boys of Tasker's School wore old-fashioned hats, turned-up long-tailed blue coats, scarlet waistcoats, corduroy breeches, yarn hose and buckled shoes, and the girls wore bonnets, white frilled caps, fichus, white aprons, turned-up blue jackets, scarlet cotton skirts, and buckled shoes. But, for me, Haverfordwest is haunted by the wistful wraith of Gwen John, sister of Augustus John, pupil of Whistler and friend of Rodin; she was a painter of delightful gifts and died at Dieppe in 1939.

A conscientious exploration of St. Bride's Bay should begin at the tip of its south-western peninsula, so remote that there is no village between Haverfordwest and Dale. On market-days the infrequent 'bus service from the town is reinforced in order that the natives of this wilderness may venture into civilisation. These 'bus-loads are primed with character, and the exiles have a distinct Scandinavian cast of countenance. The 'bus crawls in that leisurely, roundabout Welsh manner, dropping a parcel here and collecting a parcel there. It is Saturday. One small parcel addressed to the vicar of Blank provokes much speculation. The one old Viking exclaims, "Eh, we must deliver this one. Parson's sermon be in here and if he don't get it we shall have no edification tomorrow."

The village of Dale is strung along a bay inside Milford Haven. The foreshore is piled with a medley of boats, nets and lobster-pots of wickerwork. The dark fiord recedes north-eastward; in the distance the olivegreen woods of Hebrandston fall to the water's edge. The hills about are yellow with mustard. Dale is another Kenfig, though it was drowned where Kenfig was choked, for its Town Hall and cottage-terraces lie beneath the flooded meadow. In the eighteenth century or earlier it had eighteen inns and dubious houses of entertainment for the Portuguese sailors who called there. In the Middle Ages six hundred people are reputed to have died of the plague. Whatever Dale has been, and we shall never know, it is now but a small fishing community with a single inn, an over-restored church containing a font and stone altar brought from Italy in 1818, and a modern castle built on to an original fragment. From the wind-swept St. Anne's Head there is a glorious view of the Haven, its mouth marked by two lighthouses. Red sandstone cliffs here, two solitary farms, an old round tower and a wilderness of gorse.

40  Giltar Cliffs, near Tenby, Pembrokeshire

The island of Skokholm lies like a mirage upon the flat sea.   On the other side of this promontory tip is Marloes, a village even more primitive than Dale and lacking the luxury of an inn.   The bell-coted church, strangely of Welsh type, is internally whitewashed and bare, archaic enough, with long passage hagioscopes.   The struggling village consists of white-washed cottages invariably roofed with corrugated iron, and the marshy stream is overgrown with wild yellow irises.   There is here nothing of the consciously picturesque, though there is the appeal of a vigorous life reduced to elemental terms.   Formerly there was a flourishing trade in leeches collected from the now drained mere, and at one time the 'Marloes gulls', or smugglers, were notorious.

Beyond the tiny harbour known as Martin's Haven, between it and the enclosed spit of land called the Deer Park, is the island of Gateholm, a green plateau to which spring brings primroses and summer pink thrift, and which is dotted with the innumerable foundations of *cytiau*, or early stone huts.   The nearby rath, a prehistoric cliff-castle with a triple line of banks and ditches, is one of many such earthworks in the area, probably designed to throw out the Danes.   Across the wild tidal-race of Jack Sound lie the storm-lashed islands of Skomer, Skokholm and Grassholm, noted for their flora and bird-life, the gannets or solan geese and the ringing station of R. M. Lockley.   Lockley, with whom I would not compete even if I were able, has fully described these islands in several well-known and delightful books.

There are few villages on the littoral of the arc-shaped St. Bride's Bay. St. Bride's itself (the Irish St. Bridget) is a fishing village with a Norman church and a walled monastic garden said to be a relic of an early com-munity.   Little, Broad and Nolton Havens are small watering-places. Inland is Roche Castle, inhabited, a semi-circular keep with later additions and a chapel to the second storey.   It was the early home of Lucy Walters, the "brown, beautiful creature" of Evelyn's *Diary*, mistress of Charles II (she came to a worse end than "poor Nellie") and mother of the Duke of Monmouth.   Roche is really a peel-tower (from *palus*, the Latin stake) a type of fortification more common in the barmkyns of the Scottish borders.   Beyond Newgale Bridge we are once more in the 'Welshery', and the deep harbour of Solva recalls Boscastle and restores us to the Celtic norm.   Solva (37) is one of those attractive bleak places that we know so well in Cornwall, but here the cottages are whitewashed, and formerly had earthen floors engraved in patterned designs.

The road runs on to St. David's, the village which is a cathedral-city lying in the heart of a windswept, tree-less peninsula.   And beyond the miniature market-square, down the Popples, the steep lane paved with pebbles, is one of the most archaic and most romantic cathedrals in all Christendom.   It lies in a hollow of the Vallis Rosina or valley of the roses, on the edge of the wild marsh called the Dowrog and backed by the gaunt crag of Carn Llidi.   There is here nothing of Chartres, nothing

of Huysmans, and indeed little of our own English Gothic.   St. David's
(33) has a character quite its own, having some affinities perhaps with the
greater kirks of Scotland and the cathedral of St. Pol-de-Leon in Finisterre.
Here is a miniature Vatican, partly in ruins, for within this walled close
are church, episcopal palace and college.   The palace is largely the work
of that Bishop Gower who brought a hint of Italian Romanesque into
this grey country and whose arcaded parapets, seen here to perfection,
may also be seen at Lamphey and Swansea.   The buildings are of checkered stone-work, purple, cream and white, and the tracery of a great rose
window remains intact.   The purplish Caerfai stone church owes its
west front to Sir Gilbert Scott, a mere copyist who here played safe by
modelling it upon the original façade swept away by Nash.   But, with
little time to record more than a few fleeting impressions, we note the
magnificent stone choir-screen, canopied and crocketed, niched and
effigied, the unique nave roof of almost Eastern opulence, its elaborately
fretted wooden arches springing from pendants, the Romanesque arches
of the nave, which spring from peculiar Transitional and Early English
piers, the combination of triforium and clerestory, the fan-traceried
vault of the Vaughan chapel, the Celtic *olla podrida* of stone below
St. David's altar, and the reputed tombs of Giraldus and Rhys ap
Gruffydd, last native prince of South Wales.   But it is the view of the
astonishing ensemble from the Tower Gate that remains as one's abiding
memory.

The entire area of Dewisland, the 'halidom' of St. David, is amazing,
and much as I detest museum-pieces I would like to see this placed under
glass, for dire things have recently happened in Pembrokeshire.   Here,
hedges have given way to earth banks riddled with wild flowers and
crowned with gorse.   Farmhouses are of local granite stone, sometimes
whitewashed but nearly all having the same characteristics and a construction which recalls Norman technique.   Each has massive stone-
cowled chimney and round oven, a central passage from front to rear,
an ingenious use of restricted space by means of aisles, and original cheese-
press, copper and ingle-nook.   There are many such houses scattered
about this area, the most perfect examples including Rhoson Uchaf,
Hendre Einon, Llaethdy and Trefeiddan.   The purplish and reddish
cliffs of this coast, speckled with blue squill, foxgloves and bluebells, are
fretted into a number of small bays tumbling down from a Celtic monastic
desert pounded by Atlantic combers.   Indeed, a *Vitae Patrum* of early
saints in Wales remains to be written (based, perhaps, upon the *Lives* in
the Vespasian Manuscripts) and this area is closely associated with
SS. David, Patrick, Teilo, Devanus, Justinian and Non, all hermits of
Anthonian calibre.   There are ruins of chapels and hermitages dedicated
to four of them, while Justinian went one better and hid himself on
Ramsey.   The island lies beyond Ramsey Sound, a narrow but roaring
and treacherous race, the crossing of which is further threatened by the

sharp ridge of rocks feelingly called the Bitches. This is a rocky, teeth-edged island of heather dominated by two carns, formerly celebrated for its falcons and still the haunt of rare birds, while seals breed in the tunnel-like caverns.

There are few villages in the gorse-gilded country between St. David's Head and Fishguard, and it is best to explore the coast, fringed with splintered basaltic rocks and dotted with fishing hamlets at Berea, Llanrian, Trevine and Abercastell, as far as Strumble Head. The landscape eastward is dominated by the 'blue stone' crowns of the Prescelly Mountains, a wild, almost-deserted moorland whose denizens rarely come down from their stony heights. The crystalline Treffgarne rocks are southern outcrops of these hills. Isolated cottages and farms are blue-tiled and red-washed, or whitewashed like crofts in Donegal or the Hebrides. These uplands are rich in megalithic remains, of which Pentre Ifan is one of the most interesting burial-chambers in the country. Newport and bountiful Nevern are joyfully placed where the Nevern river enters Newport Bay. From here the way to Cardigan is via Eglwyswrw, with its old Sergeant's Arms inn and its church containing a Sienese paten of cinquecento work, or, preferably, by way of St. Dogmael's, a fishing village loitering along the shore of the Teifi estuary. Here are the scanty remains of an abbey which belonged to the Tironesian reform and to which Caldey was affiliated; the infirmary chapel has some thirteenth-century details and one arch has good ball-flower ornament.

Across the bridge is Cardigan. It is November, and 'Shoni Onions', the Breton onion-seller, has just made his annual appearance.

St. David's Cathedral: the Nave and Screen
*From a drawing by Walter Crane*

# VI

## THE TEIFI VALLEY    CARDIGAN COAST
## RHEIDOL AND YSTWYTH VALLEYS
## PLYNLIMON    ABERYSTWYTH

IT were ill-advised in speaking to a 'Cardi', or native of Cardiganshire, to refer to Cardigan as the county town, for the distinction is also claimed by Aberystwyth and Lampeter, the former having the head-quarters of the county council and the latter the assizes. Indeed, Cardigan has little enough dignity left it, and its port is obsolete, for the estuary is silted up, though fishermen yet put out and use the seine net. Nash's county gaol has gone, two ruined drum-towers alone remain of the castle, and the Three Mariners Inn, with its Jacobean woodwork and enriched ceilings, has recently been demolished. Yet the town is beautifully situated upon the Teifi and the vistas from its seven-arched bridge are appealing. The church has a fine buttressed tower and an east window with perfect tracery, though most of the original glass was probably removed to Hafod by Thomas Johnes, who owned the priory house here. The excellent late Gothic chancel is a remnant of a Benedictine priory and was obviously completed just prior to the Dissolution; here is an unusually good piscina with crocketed ogee arch and a conventional rose sculptured upon the bowl, while a corbel is carved with the head of a woman in late fifteenth-century head-dress. Nearby are small monastic gatehouse and Priory House, now a hospital. The latter was the home of Catherine Phillips, friend of Restoration literati and the Orinda of *Letters from Orinda to Poliarchus*; it was rebuilt by Nash in the Gothic of the period, but is now shorn of porch and embattlements.

But we have already arrived at Llechryd, with its neat old bridge over the Teifi (42) and its tiny church, in which a coracle is kept handy (in the porch) to fish some unfortunate out of the river. There is a nice composi-tion made up of the bridge and the early-Victorian neo-Jacobean lodge of Castell Maelgwyn. The house is a severe eighteenth-century mansion built for Sir Benjamin Hammett, a Lombard Street banker, though in 1848 plans were drawn up for a more ambitious estate. By courtesy of the owner I was privileged to see the original plans and drawings, by Ambrose Poynter, who was a founder member of the Royal Institute of

42  The Bridge over the Teifi at Llechryd, Cardiganshire

43  Coracle Fishermen under the Bridge at Cenarth, Cardiganshire

44　The Beach at Aberporth, Cardiganshire

45　Pen-y-Gareg Reservoir in the Elan Valley, Radnorshire

British Architects, architect to the National Provincial Bank of England, attended Keats' funeral in Rome, and was the father of a more famous son. These drawings show an ornate house somewhat resembling Thoresby in the Sherwood Forest (designed by Salvin just twenty years later), a range of out-buildings containing coach-house, laundry, etc., and a lodge. The house was never built. What remains are the lodge and out-building, but the latter is itself an intriguing affair with quadrangular ranges with mullioned windows, corbie-stepped gables, an ogee-shaped cupola and a saddlebacked tower containing a chime of bells. A stream encloses it on two sides, and the result is a moated palace such as may be seen upon the Dyver in Bruges. There is here a suggestion of failure or perhaps decadence, the half-derelict buildings, the salmon weigh-house, no longer functional, the abandoned tin-works and slate quarries, though the latter are not to be seen in the park itself.

There is a private path through the park to the banks of the Teifi, which here describes an arc and may be followed to Cilgerran. This section of the river flows through a dramatic wooded gorge, deserted save for a few birds startled into agitated flight. The path is narrow and rocky, slimy and rather hazardous in the wet season. There are abandoned slate-workings and an occasional coracle lying inverted, like a giant tortoise, upon the bank. Soon the broken castle of Cilgerran is seen dominating the heights in a setting which compelled Richard Wilson, Peter de Wint, David Cox and Turner to bring palettes and brushes. From the castle itself the valley is a blaze of autumn glory in which, almost inevitably, appears the summer-house of a Georgian mansion in the woods upon the far bank. The original Cilgerran is dubiously said to have been built by that Robert Montgomery who is reputed to have led the van of the Normans at Hastings. The existing structure had two wards, but little remains beyond two drum-towers and fragments of the curtain. In the village are old stone cottages and inn and a church which contains a Latin and Ogham stone. At nearby Bridell Carmelite nuns maintain the Teresian *Opus Dei*. Sandalled and leather-girdled, in habits of brown cloth with black veiling over white wimples, they are strictly enclosed and rarely taste the delights of these aromatic lanes.

Between here and Cenarth, in the hamlet of Abercych, wood-turning is yet done by the primitive pole-lathe (as it is in the Chilterns and the Forest of Dean). The tradition of excellent craftsmanship has here been in the same family for generations. The products, bowls, trenchers, ladles, spoons, etc., are of traditional design and have characteristics found in similar work among the Central European lake-dwellers, particularly in the hooked tips of ladle and spoon handles. The woods used are syca-more, walnut, cherry, oak and yew, largely from those local trees in which the Teifi valley is rich, though a little oak is imported from England. There was until recently another such wood-turning centre at Henlan, as there was at Llanrhystyd a factory for the manufacture of woollen yarn, conducted by early methods. Baskets are yet made by hand at Ffostrassol and coracles are made at Cenarth. All these places are within our area. The men of Cardiganshire are craftsmen, and in this area we have yet a vision of what the honest proletariat was before the Industrial Revolution and the current wave of Socialism seduced him into a pampered and superficially educated work-shy, tawdry smart-Alec.

Cenarth up-river, with its bridge and rapids, its inn with round-headed windows in painted black archibolts and its church with curious grotesques upon the font-bowl, is one of the very few places in which coracles are made (though as late as a decade ago they were made at Bewdley on the Severn). The coracle is the *vitilia navigia* of Pliny and the craft of Herodotus. It is the Donegal *curragh* and the *curach* of the Boyne river in County Meath, and it is the first cousin of the skin-covered vessel used in southern India and on the Yang-tse-Kiang. The Welsh coracle, used in ever-declining measure on the Teifi, Towy, Cleddau, Cothi, Dee and Wye, is constructed rather differently from the hide-bound craft of Ireland and is made of a lathwork of ash and hazel covered with tarred calico. The craft is trickily navigated by a paddle, the fishermen working in pairs with a net suspended between two coracles (43). These fishermen are so adept with their primitive craft that they here use them to advantage for sheep-washing in the river. Their sense of adventure and profit has, however, led them to misuse their craft, poaching and catching salmon and sea trout, here called sewin, by illegal means. Consequently the law has forbidden the privilege of using coracles to be handed down to future generations. Soon there will be no more coracles on Teifi.

Newcastle Emlyn, where the Teifi makes a majestic sweep which surrounds the ruined castle with a superb natural moat, has little of the dramatic composition seen in the watercolour by Ibbetson, though it is yet possible to find such a cottage kitchen as was engraved by Rowlandson. I have encountered beautiful bookbindings by Thomas Jones, a local craftsman who flourished early last century. There is little enough of interest now, but one has glimpses of an earlier life of grace and leisure, and the cockle vendor still cries his wares. The first printing-press in Wales was set up here in 1719 and the town was a focal point of the Chartist 'Rebecca' Riots, when enraged mobs clad in female attire attacked toll-houses and gates, shrewdly justifying their actions by a text from Genesis. Allen Raine (Anne Adeliza Evans who became Mrs. Beyuon Puddecombe), a best-seller of the latter part of last century, was a native and resident of this town. The vogue for her books, regional novels which exploited the romantic concept and portrayed a false Wales, has happily passed. The nearby hamlet of Henlan, with fine old bridge, rapids and the manor-house of Llysnewydd (Nash again, but completely altered) in the fields above, is a more plausible slice of Wales.

Llandyssul's single street climbs above the river, a Crucifixion carved upon the façade of the church and the churchyard stone-banked at the water's edge. Caradoc Evans, first of the dynasty of modern Welsh short-story writers, was born near here. He was apprenticed to drapers in Carmarthen and Cardiff (in Wales haberdashery and literature seem curiously linked), picked up English in London, became a Fleet Street journalist and startled the Principality out of its lethargy with sordid satires of Welsh life. This is the country of *My People, Capel Sion* and *Taffy*, the play which nearly wrecked a London theatre.

Lampeter, with its horse-fair and theological college, is the capital of Teifi-side. St. David's College (47) was founded in 1822 in order to provide Welsh clergy for the Established Church; it has a quasi-university status, and its students, unlike those of the University of Wales, live in college and dine in hall. Cockerell has here produced an attractive and convincing replica of an Oxford college, neo-Gothic, its chapel filled with enriched woodwork and stalls with coved canopy, all in scarlet, green and gilt. The old grammar school here also had some academic reputation, and there must have been substantial grounds for Sir Walter Scott to send his son to such an outlandish place. The church is modern, but there are a few late Georgian façades, such as the black-and-white Lion Hotel. Outside the town is a fragment of Peterwell, which once had four domed towers and a roof-garden, the eighteenth-century home of that Sir Herbert Lloyd who was one of the vilest scoundrels ever to disgrace a Welsh landscape.

From Lampeter a detour can be made along the fertile valley of the Aeron to Aberayron on the coast, a small seaport which has declined into a watering-place, and in which most of the houses date from about 1807 and have characteristics of that period. Llanarth church, with lions sculptured about the base of an early font, and the farmhouse of Wern, which sheltered Henry VII on his way to Bosworth, may be seen en route for New Quay, with its twin bays and its harbour tumbling down below the wooded hills. Here the churchyard is filled with memorials to lost mariners, fine sea-dogs who had rounded the Horn in the days of sail. This is a coast of much grandeur, and in it, between New Quay and Cardigan, are squeezed the fishing villages of Llangranog, Penbryn and Traethsaeth.

Beyond Lampeter, the silver mines of Llanfair Clydogau and the site of the *Luentium* of Ptolemy, is the village of Llanddewi Brefi, linked with some pretty if dubious legends of St. David, who, however, certainly came here and contracted a headache in confuting the Pelagians of the period. The thirteenth-century church of St. David is large but plain and shorn of its transepts, and there are three primitive Celtic crosses in the churchyard. William of Wykeham was a prebendary here. Tregaron, on a tributary of the Teifi, is a "very good place; not quite so big as London, but very good place", a place, moreover, celebrated for "very good ham" and for "great man, clever thief, Twm Shon Catti, who was born there". But we cannot let Borrow have the last word, for, contrary to his own opinion, I know of nothing less Spanish than Tregaron —and nothing more Welsh. The market square is dominated by the bronze statue of Henry Richard, invariably dubbed 'advocate of international arbitration' but also a man who compelled Westminster to realise the plight of Wales last century. Victorian frock-coated, spectacles in hand, adopting an oratorical stance, he undoubtedly looks more statesman than Congregational minister. The church of St. Carron, the bells of Strata Florida ringing from its massive tower splayed at the base, stands in a circular churchyard. From the back of the town, eastward, runs the mountain track to the Towy valley and Abergwesyn, wild country which is one of the last breeding-places in Britain of the kite. This is the most considerable uninhabited moorland wilderness south of the Scottish highlands or Galloway, extending east to Abergwesyn, from the Trumau hills and the Claerwen river, flowing to the Elan reservoirs in the north, to Twm Shon Catti's cave in the south. It is an empty land of green, tumbled, rolling hills and winding streams, with heathery moorland, rocky outcrops and bogs, of some 300 square miles, a dissected plateau of Silurian grits and shales, ranging in height from about 1,000 feet in the river clefts up to some 1,700 on the hills, with one or two little pieces over the 2,000 feet level, as at Drygarn Fawr, north of Abergwesyn, a fine view-point. It seems nameless, but Giraldus refers to it as 'Ellenith', a term it is now sought to revive. The area, shared between the shires of Cardigan, Radnor and Carmarthen, is bisected by the upper waters of the Towy flowing nearly due south, and most of the scanty, lonely habitations, largely sheep farms, are dotted about the river and its tributaries. A rough track from Strata Florida joining the course of the Towy brings the adventurous traveller finally to Llandovery, and cutting across it is the drovers' road from Tregaron to Abergwesyn, a splendid way to follow, but by no means suitable for cars. Beyond the town stretches Cors Caron, the Bog of Tregaron, a vast area of peat haunted by grouse, snipe and teal, a sombre, melancholy landscape with its inevitable folk-tale of a buried city, Maesllyn.

Northward, the Teifi rises in trout-pools high up in the hills. We have tracked it to its source and so must leave it. One must make a brief detour to see the ruins of Ystrad Flur, the Cistercian abbey of Strata Florida. Little remains of this celebrated and intensely Welsh monastery, but the conventual church has been fully excavated. The ruins are late Norman and Transitional in character, and the major feature is the Romanesque west doorway recessed in five bands of moulding, highly original in design and early Irish in inspiration. The transeptal chapels have encaustic tiles *in situ* and there are a number of conventual graves marked with perfect head-crosses. Dafydd ap Gwilym, greatest of all Welsh poets and perhaps as brilliant a personality as his contemporaries

46 Laura Place, Aberystwyth. Late eighteenth-century

St. David's College, Lampeter, Cardiganshire, designed by C. R. Cockerell in 1826
*From Jones' "Views" (1829)*

48 Hafod, Cardiganshire.  Designed c. 1785 by Baldwin of Bath.  Later additions by John Nash and Harrison of Chester

Chaucer and Dante, is reputed to lie here. The old Welsh annals, *Brut y Tywysogion*, were in part compiled here, and Henry IV in his pursuit of Glyndowr stalled his horses at the high altar and then sacked the abbey. We see the immature, struggling Teifi for the last time as we cross the bridge at Pontrhydfendigaed and make for the valley of the Ystwyth via Yspytty Ystwyth.

Hafod, the Welsh Strawberry Hill, that strange house above the Ystwyth, is now a melancholy ruin in a glory of woodland. It was built in 1785 by Thomas Johnes, who fell a victim of the Romantic cult. His architect was Baldwin of Bath, who here created a 'Gothick' pavilion with embellishments savouring of the Moorish (48). The octagonal library with coffered dome opening on to a conservatory dominated by Banks' sculpture of *Thetis dipping Achilles into the Styx* was the *chef-d'œuvre* of a mansion crammed with such exotic curiosa as tables of lava from Vesuvius, a fragment of Pompey's column from Alexandria, Gobelin tapestries, etc. The library included the Pesaro Library from Venice, a collection which was being catalogued in London at the time of the disastrous fire in 1807 and was fortunately preserved (many of these volumes were on sale in London in 1940). Here too Johnes set up his celebrated printing-press and published his own translations of Froissart, de Joinville, Bertrandon de la Brocquière, Monstrelet, etc., in editions of much *éclat*. He threw elaborate parties and illuminated the best scenic features by Bengal lights. But he was no autocrat and was at loggerheads with local mis-government, and when Napoleon threatened an invasion Johnes made a speech which delighted Coleridge: "House plundered, then burnt, sons conscribed, wives and daughters ravished . . . but as for you, you luxurious Aldermen! with *your* fat will he grease the wheels of his triumphal chariot." At Hafod Johnes set up a thriving centre of agriculture and the arts, and he was the ideal landlord. He built cottages, school and apothecary for his tenants and frequently entertained them inside the mansion. He wrote, published and distributed a pamphlet *A Cardiganshire Landlord's Advice to his Tenants*, settled Scottish farmers on the estate, and at one time planned to import a hundred Swiss families from the Grisons. No such landlords will be found under the new regime, except those of the old school, who are being steadily crushed and exiled by the new chaos. Most of the original Hafod was destroyed in 1807, but was rebuilt by Nash and, later, Harrison of Chester. But the final touches, *mirabile dictu*, were added by Salvin, who here raised Italianate campanile and terraces, while the nearby church (since rebuilt) was designed by Wyatt and contained a monument by Chantrey. Hafod is thus the composite work of six major craftsmen, Baldwin of Bath, John Nash, Harrison of Chester, James Wyatt, Anthony Salvin and Chantrey, and few estates in the country can claim such a distinction. Now all is lost, scorched and derelict.

Since we are in the placid valley of the Ystwyth we may follow the

7**

river through miles of rhododendrons to another once-celebrated library. Crosswood, formerly a seat of Viscount Lisburne, stands in a sylvan park facing the scarped hills. The buildings are largely Victorian but the nucleus has an eighteenth-century façade with armorial pediment and Ionic porch, the volutes curiously deformed. The library is a highly festive apartment framed by Corinthian fluted columns supporting cornice and richly panelled ceiling divided up by bands of guilloche and other enrichments. The central panel is slightly coved and frescoed with cherubin, and the side panels have floral medallions, each containing a bas-relief of an angel in flight carrying infants. Gilded anthemion is the *motif* employed in the pediments of the doorcases, in the overmantel and bookcases. The latter, which housed many volumes once belonging to John Selden of *Table Talk*, are ranged around the walls and have open screening of gilt filigree work. The gilt and crystal chandelier and the three-light convex bay opening on to the garden, the arched windows in gilded architraves and draped with heavy damask curtains, enhance this colourful picture, but the original decorative scheme was much extended late last century and is now florid and congested, rather as though a Pugin in the pagan tradition had gone beserk.

From Pontrhydygroes beyond Hafod there is a choice of roads to Devil's Bridge, the more attractive climbing high above the Mynach. I have always been sceptical of 'fairy glens' *et id genus omne*, but Devil's Bridge as the focal point of some magnificent scenery is truly one of the major delights of Wales. This miniature paradise is contained within the grounds of a hotel which has rooms with startling views and which formerly provided Victorian ladies visiting the falls with "an elegant and appropriate Garibaldian or Turkish flannel costume". The ravine down which the Mynach pours into the Rheidol is spanned by the Pont y Monach, the Monk's Bridge, a single arch thrown over another of earlier date and superstitiously ascribed to the Devil, as is the bridge over the Reuss at Lucerne and as is the Roman Devil's Wall in Germany. The gloomy abyss is hung with fretted skeins of water in four progressive falls culminating in a grand cataract, and the spray breaks about velvet rocks and reflects the prismatic colours. There are other falls at Nant Lettys and Cyfarllwyd. Higher up the glorious Rheidol valley, just below the bell-coted church of Yspytty Cynfin, is the Parson's Bridge, for the secular clergy cannot be outdone by the regular. South-westward stretches the lonely mountain road, broken by numerous little *afons*, to Rhayader and the Elan valley (45). It is a grim, desolate country tenanted only by shepherds and their flocks, and I have been content to throw myself down for a night in a deserted barn near the hamlet of Tyllwyd. Yet farther north is the sodden wilderness of Plynlimon, the high tableland of bog and shale with a summit which is ill-defined and always tantalisingly elusive and the watershed of numerous streams. In its plover-haunted recesses five rivers have their mystic sources, the Severn,

Wye, Rheidol, Llyfnant and Clywedog.   It is best attacked from the inn
of Dyffryn Castell and may also be gained by a track from Llanidloes to
the east.   Though it has neither the character nor appeal of Snowdon,
Cader Idris or the Carmarthen Van there are those who are sensitive to
its charms, and it is perhaps the Cinderella of all our mountains.

But clearly we have been wilfully avoiding Aberystwyth for too long
and now hasten along the direct road from Devil's Bridge.   But beyond
Capel Sion we are halted in the valley of the infant Paith by the park of
Nanteos, perhaps the most beautiful estate in the shire.   The ancient hall
was rebuilt in the eighteenth century and has a curious centrepiece with
three tall, round-headed windows, three circular lights above and a
colonnaded porch below.   This scene was once further enriched by the
green-eyed and flaming-haired figure of Swinburne, a frequent guest of
his friend, George Powell.   Francophil and Pre-Raphaelite, a declaimer
against Christianity, he must have cut a strange figure in Victorian Wales.
And here is yet kept the Holy Grail of Wales, a miraculous cup reputedly
made from a piece of the True Cross and originally at Strata Florida.

Contrary to popular opinion, Aberystwyth is not one of the *nouveaux
riches* among watering-places, for it was fashionable at least as early as
Regency Brighton, with which indeed it has much affinity.   Moreover,
this is the cultural centre of this western world.   There are here some
delightful architectural studies, and there must be more Georgian houses
than in any other Welsh town.   Good Ionic and Doric doorcases, some
of them convex with triglyphs engraved upon the cornices, may be seen
in Great Dark Gate Street, where is the Lion Royal with scarlet engraved
stucco-work, windows in cream moulded architraves and a porch with
green, fluted wood shafts.   In Bridge Street are several modest bow
windows, the Black Lion with twisted barley-sugar fluting to the entrance
pillars, and the severe eighteenth-century town-houses of the Pryses of
Gogerddan, now a newspaper office.   This last is of grey stone with tall
windows and an Ionic doorcase with fanlight and panelled soffits. Almost
opposite is a similar house with Ionic porch of less elegant proportions,
the fat, ungainly pillars having massive volutes.   In Pier Street are some
elegant examples of the Regency with double-fronted bow windows,
tiered over three storeys.   A delightful characteristic of the town is the
number of windows in moulded architraves terminating above in little
curls and quite resembling Baroque mirrors.   The Baroque may also
be detected in the twin towers of Siloh Chapel.   There is, of course, a
clan of these Victorian chapels, one of them designed by Butterfield,
though there is little enough to speak for him.

The oasis of Aberystwyth is Laura Place, where are the earliest urbane
houses of the town, sedate homes which have borrowed not a little from
Adam (46).   Here too is the college refectory, a low, hipped-roofed
pavilion with gables and arched windows, built in 1820 to designs by
Stanley Repton and formerly the Assembly Rooms with all the pomps

and routs of Bath under Beau Nash.   The centre of the square is occupied
by the parish church, the work of Sir Thomas Nicholson (who designed
three churches in Swansea), neat, correct and convincing Gothic with
perfect window tracery but chilly and unexciting.   And facing all this is
the University College, as out of place here as a surrealistic drop-curtain
to a Romney—and rather like it.   Its history is almost as fantastic as its
contours.   The original, designed by Nash for Sir Uvedale Price,
Etonian, Herefordshire squire and landscape-gardener, was little better
than a Batty Langley sham and savoured of *fin-de-siècle* Romanticism.
In 1864 this Castle House was bought by a manager of the Cambrian
Railway, who with the aid of Seddon, the architect, converted it into
a hotel.   The funds gave out before the ambitious buildings were completed, and the site was taken over at a most opportune moment by a
committee who were about to found a national university.   Seddon was
recalled, the bar-parlour became the college chapel, the billiard-room
became the library and the ballroom became the examination-hall.   A
few years later much of the building was destroyed by fire, and Seddon
was again called in to complete the final metamorphosis of this extravaganza.   Seddon, like his partner John Pritchard of Llandaff, followed
Ruskin, and what we see here is a bastardised form of Venetian Gothic,
with an entrance porch which recalls the London Law Courts and two
lofty round towers which might have been imported from Portugal.
Within there is the same whimsical riot, heraldic roofs, twisted staircases,
mysterious mosaics and a covered quadrangle dominated by the giant
figure of Lord Aberdare, the gallery pierced with quatrefoils.

   Indeed we have left ourselves little time in which to see the fragments
of the diamond-shaped castle, to fondle the early manuscripts of Chaucer
and the *Roman de la Rose* in the National Library, and to stroll along the
promenade strung like a ribbon along Cardigan Bay.   At Llanbadarn
Fawr we shall find the mother-church of this town which lives a dual life,
the church of the Breton St. Paternus, largely thirteenth-century with
massive central tower, Early English lancets, Perpendicular chancel,
Celtic crosses and the grave of Lewis Morris, the poet.   Near Llangorwen
on the road to Borth is Cwm Cynfelyn, the Georgian house in which the
pious Keble frequently stayed.   Keble's influence may be seen in Llangorwen itself, where the church is a near-replica of Newman's church
at Littlemore outside Oxford.   Gogerddan, the ancient seat of the Pryses,
is near here, but it has been much rebuilt.   Across the golden-broom
hills, beyond the flannel-mills of Tal-y-Bont, is the *kistvaen* of Bedd
Taliesin, traditionally the grave of Taliesin, the earliest of Welsh bards
(though he was really British), who died in the sixth century at the close
of an earlier civilisation.

   It is nightfall, and we may prefer to spend the night in Aberystwyth.
In Laura Place we may fancy that we see the members of the Cym-
morodorion Society in their green-and-red-striped coon trousers.   But

no, except for an occasional black-gowned figure flitting about the precincts of the yellow-stone college the place is deserted. For it is winter. A few weeks more will see the end of term. The tanned parchment faces of old ladies peer from boarding-house casements. The hills are dotted with brilliant greenish-yellow lights like glow-worms, and all along the front there comes the furtive sough of the sea.

The Basset and Mansel Tomb, Llanrithyd, Glamorganshire

# VII

## BRECON AND THE BEACONS
## THE USK VALLEY    THE BLACK MOUNTAINS
## THE RADNOR FOREST    THE UPPER WYE

ABERHONDDU, *anglice* Brecon, is cradled between the hills, set astride the Usk and its more musical tributary the Honddu, that trickles past the village of Llanddew, where Giraldus Cambrensis as a young archdeacon gazed from the episcopal palace upon the mist-nimbed Pen-y-fan.   I am inclined to regard this uplandish old county town as the most delightful in Wales—and the least known.   It is laved by a trinity of rivers, whose singing waters lulled me to sleep during the icy nights of the savage winter of 1946–47, when the Beacons were impassable and the few farmers who made their way into the town were melancholy and tight-lipped, and when local cattle losses mounted daily. But Brecon in spring is sheer joy, embowered in bountiful trees from which birds cry Hosanna on the champagne-bright morning.   It is then one thinks of Henry Vaughan, greatest of all our Christian Platonists, to whom you may here pay homage, for his ancestors lived at Newton Manor, and he himself married and practised as a physician here, often taking his constitutional among the beeches of the Priory Groves.   And I like to think of this as Brangwyn country, since the painter's mother came from a local farmhouse.   Sir Frank tells me that his father came from Marlow (though his ancestors were Welsh), while his mother was 'a pure Celt'.   Thus a dual strain runs through Brangwyn's work, for, in spite of the Flemish elements, his opulent, robust colour, his symbolism and sensuousness of line are in the Celtric tradition.

Brecon was originally a town of timber-framed houses, and the forerunner of the present Town Hall was attributed to John Abel, King's Carpenter, who did so much good work in Herefordshire.   Much early fabric remains.   The Georgian Constabulary has yet a Gothic quatrefoiled panel above a fireplace and a modern café retains a seventeenth-century heraldic panel.   The face of the town is largely Georgian; there is the Queen-Anne-type County Club, the Y.M.C.A. building with Venetian windows, the yellow-ochre washed Castle Hotel, where George IV dined, and the Regency pharmacy with Corinthian columns and arabesques beneath the windows. We have only to look at the staircases to see that some of these buildings are architectural palimpsests. An uninteresting façade in Glamorgan Street conceals panelled powder- ing-rooms and a staircase with 'barley-sugar' turned balusters. There are excellent Jacobean staircases in the George Inn, Old Oak Tea Rooms, Punch Bowl Hotel and Church House, and many of slightly later date in the High Street and elsewhere. I have seen a score of them and there must be others. Brecon undoubtedly possesses the finest collection of staircases in the entire Principality. Other local characteristics include tiled floors, slate-hung outer walls and early-Victorian three-light shop- fronts.

In the eighteenth and early nineteenth centuries the local squirearchy built town houses in Brecon, thus creating a Little Season. At one time Sir Charles Morgan lived at Ely Cottage in the shadow of the castle, the Reverend Sir John Thomas lived nearby, the Marquess Camden lived at The Priory, an ancestor of the present Viscount Tredegar lived at Mansion House (recently demolished) and Lancelot Morgan lived at Morganwyg House (now a convent: I remember a beautiful young nun who took me through the convent parlours and walked with me in the garden banked up on the old city-wall which stays the Usk in flood). There was a Theatre Royal which had its announcements printed on silk, and tobacco was grown in fragrant gardens. Slightly later generations of Breconians could drink gloriously until they were cock-eyed, for a century ago there were ninety inns in the small town. In the cathedral you may notice the grave of Thomas Longfellow, host of the Golden Lion in coaching days.

Above the Honddu, the back doors of cottages opening *on to* the water, is the cathedral of old red sandstone brocaded with blue harebells. The grim fortress-like priory church, founded by Bernard de Neufmarche in order "to pave his way to Heaven", has an internal beauty unsuspected from without (49). It is well proportioned, and the Early English quintuplet lancets in the admirable chancel, with graduated triplets at the sides, are among the finest of their period. The chancel vault, however, is the work of Sir Gilbert Scott and (for Scott) exceedingly well done. The extremely rare triple piscina, the almost equally rare rosary carved upon an early tomb, and an ancient cresset are things to be noted. The tradition of good craftsmanship is brought into our own century by Sir William Goscombe John's [1] noble effigied tomb of Bishop Bevan and

---

[1] Born in Cardiff in 1860. He was early influenced by Rodin, whom he watched at work in Paris, corresponded with Constantin Meunier and was a contemporary and friend of Burne-Jones and the Pre-Raphaelites, Lord Leighton, Clausen, Sargent, Woolner, Alfred Gilbert and others. Though he admires the Gothic tradition, in which his Brecon work is an essay, his work is mainly in the Classical idiom and may be seen in St. Paul's, Westminster Abbey and many of the cathedrals. He is a prolific worker of international repute, and his war memorials are encountered in London, Cairo, Bagdhad, Calcutta and the provinces. Though he has executed

by his carved episcopal throne.   The note of originality is extended to
the capitular buildings, of which the nucleus is the canonry, formerly the
monastic guest-house and later a Stuart coach-house and stable.   W. D.
Caröe was responsible for this novel transformation, and in these handsome
vestries the original manger-posts with their tethering-rings, hoof-marks
and tallow-burns have been retained.   The deanery or Priory House was
the home of that Sir John Price who has hitherto been regarded as the man
who drafted the petition which resulted in the abolition of the Marches
and the Union of England and Wales, for Professor Gwyn Jones tells me
that Welsh scholars no longer hold this view.   But the celebrated Golden
Rood of Brecon has gone and few pilgrims climb the steep grey hill to
Evensong, when the dean and a minor canon, reading the lesson, their
white surplices illumined by a single light, stand alone amid the shadowy
recesses.

The castle, merged into a Georgian hotel, retains an embattled great
hall and the Ely tower, so-called since Morton, Bishop of Ely, was
imprisoned there in 1483, though these buildings are some two centuries
earlier in date.   Morton, later a cardinal, incited his gaoler, the second
Duke of Buckingham, to secede from the cause of Richard III and to
overthrow him.   The venture fared ill—as did all three Dukes of
Buckingham, Lords of Brecknock—and the duke was executed.   His
father had fallen in the cause of Lancaster at the Battle of Northampton,
and his son, a victim of Wolsey's intrigues, was to perish on the block.
It was this third and last Stafford lord who built the fine tower of the
parish church, a tower which cost a thousand pounds of fifteenth-century
currency and on which, high upon the stringcourse, is moulded the
Stafford Knot.   The church itself contains little beyond an unusual
dog-door and an early coffin-lid incised with arrow-heads and probably
from an archer's tomb, for Brecknock archers were formidable, as the
French learned at Agincourt, but the font is the one at which the immortal
Sarah Siddons was baptised; the pent-up unlighted room in which she
was born remains unaltered in the Shoulder of Mutton inn.

Over Llanfaes Bridge, across the quick-glinting Usk with sycamore-
and poplar-lined banks, is Christ's College, an essay in Venetian Gothic
by Pritchard of Llandaff, though it embodies the refectory, a chamber used
as a library and the thirteenth-century choir of a Dominican friary.   The
last, now the school chapel, has lovely triple lancets and local squires
petrified in Roman togas, among them the Lucys, a branch of the family
we encounter in Shakespeare's Forest of Arden.   On the far bank of the
Tarell, which here plunges into the Usk, is Newton Manor, humble now
but retaining its great hall, a crested overmantel dated 1582 with Welsh
inscription, and fragments of a gallery.   Sir David Gam, who saved

numerous smaller works in Wales, his work is best judged by the collection in the
National Museum, which includes such original and vigorous sculptures as *The
Drummer Boy*, *The Elf* and *St. John the Baptist*.

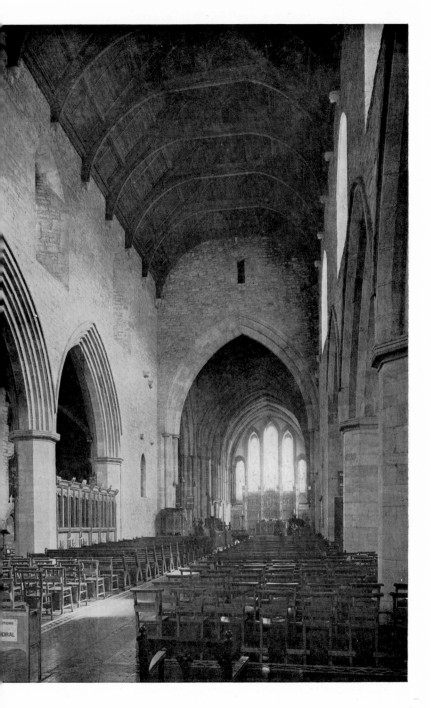

49   Brecon Cathedral : the Nave and Choir

50 The Brecon Beacons

51 Near Chirbury, Montgomeryshire, with Corndon Hill (1684 ft.) behind

Henry V at Agincourt and was probably the original of Shakespeare's Fluellen, lived either here or at Aberbran.

The road from Llanfaes to Llandovery flirts with the Usk and is flanked by the moorlands of the Mynydd Epynt northward and the mountainous Fforest Fawr to the south. At Llanspyddyd, where the fourteenth-century church contains a curious canopy above the pulpit, is the grave of Amlwch, the bard. Beyond the medieval bridge and Tudor farm-house of Aberbran and the yew-trees of Capel Bettws is Penpont. The house has a colonnaded portico and, it is said, memories of Anne Boleyn, whose portrait, *triste* and doe-eyed, graces the rich interior. The pigeon-cote is characteristic of this area, not of the round columbarium type but rectangular, with a passage-way cut through the lower storey and crowned with a whimsical conical lantern. The cedars and firs cluster thickly about Scott's neo-Norman chapel. By night it is a dark, lonely spot. There is a reputedly true story of a local man accompanied by his wife both of them on horseback, returning home from the taverns of Brecon some forty years ago. Approaching this place they saw what appeared to be a white figure hovering beneath the trees. The horses too were alarmed, for they came to a halt and could be urged no farther. He was a timid man, but not without resources. He looked the apparition or whatever it was in the face and said: "If you are the Lord I know you won't harm me, for my brother is vicar of a parish in Pembrokeshire. And if you be the Devil you surely won't harm me, for I'm living with your sister."

Abercamlais, the next mansion on Usk-side, was built in 1571, the very year of Aberyscir on the far bank, though both have been somewhat altered. The pigeon-cote of Abercamlais is similar to that of Penpont, but the most remarkable feature here is the eighteenth-century privy over a stream, an arrangement providing six seats, three for the family and three for the servants, with a single dividing wall. Trecastle, with its single street of whitewashed cottages, lies ahead, but we must return to Brecon and the Beacons.

The Beacons reach high heaven in Pen-y-fan and Corn-Ddu, the indigo corniced throne of an intriguing moorland (50). The best ascents from Brecon are the direct ones via the Gribyn, the smaller peak eastward, and via the long ridge of Cwn-Ilwch beyond the shepherd's cottage. There is a dark, leech-filled tarn cradled among the hills, and red scree lies below the summit. The massif may also be attacked from Storey Arms on the new Merthyr road, a scenic way ending in the gloom of Merthyr, though you may turn off at the first reservoir and take the moorland road across the Hepste river to the remote hamlet of Ystradfellte. Here the Mellte pours along its rocky bed, fringed with beech and ash, and nearby the river plunged in a spectacular torrent over a limestone ravine to disappear into the arched cavern of Porth-yr-Ogof, which the natives say is bottomless. Some way below lie the upper, middle and lower

Clyngwyn falls, of which the middle fall is crescent-shaped, and near the junction of the Mellte and Hepste is a grand culminating cataract. The upper falls of the Hepste project forward so much that one may pass behind the watery screen. North-eastward of Ystradfellte runs the Sarn Helen, a remote Roman causeway which joins the mountain road above the Afon Llia. Follow this as far as you wish, but do not stray from its course, for this is a grim inhospitable land, uninhabited and awesome, yet with its own strange perverse beauty. It is a corrugated land riddled with primitive memorials, untenanted save for the curlew, the dunlin and the golden plover flying low above the cotton-grass. Below, in the valley of the Senni, is a road which may be followed to the Cray reservoir in the valley of the Tawe where trout swim between pale limestone cliffs. Below Glyntawe lies Craig-y-nos, an Italianate mountain eyrie lying in the shadow of the naked Carmarthen Van. This was the home of the Baroness Cederström, better known as Madame Patti, the opera singer, and nearby is Callwen church, where she worshipped and which contains one of the rare Georgian three-decker pulpits of Wales. An acquaintance of mine went to the sale following Madame Patti's death and paid £9 (1919 currency) for a rare copy of Theophilus Jones' *History of Brecknock*—and someone filched it from him on the same day.

From Brecon the Usk sweeps eastward to the purlieus of the Black Mountains (52), and the main road to Crickhowel skirts the northern bank. Beyond the rebuilt church of Llanhamlach, where is an early Christian stone sculptured with the Virgin and St. John, is Scethrog, the Tudor manor-house in which lived Henry Vaughan and in which his words are carved above a fireplace: *To God, Thy Father and thy Land Be True*. Here too is the Victorinus stone, one of the many Roman and sub-Roman stones in which Brecknock is so rich, many of which are related to the Ogham stones, those with Gaelic inscriptions based upon the Roman alphabet mainly of fifth- and sixth-century date and of south-Irish inspiration. There are carved and inscribed Roman stones near Aberyscir, at Llanfrynach, Devynock, Llywel, Llangorse, Llanspyddid, Llandefaelog, the Peregrinus stone at Tretower, the Catacus stone at Llanfihangel Cwndu, the Turpillan stone in Glanusk Park and many others. This is indeed a land of riches, and at Llansantffraed (56), near a wild strawberry-bed in the churchyard, lies Vaughan, *Henricus Vaughan Silurens*. Through the Bwlch cutting ("Once through Bwlch Pass a Welshman never returns", lies an old proverb) and beyond the larch-covered hill of Myarth a by-road leads to Tretower amid the apple orchards. Tretower Court was the ancestral home of the Vaughan family, but the architectural qualities of the building eclipse, for the moment, any thoughts of the poet lingering in our minds, for this early-fifteenth-century fortified manor-house is a major example of the transition from castle to country house, having much affinity with Stokesay in Shropshire. Today it is a national monument, completely restored,

52   An Upland Landscape in the Black Mountains, near Partrishow, Brecknockshire

53   Llanfilo, near Brecon

54   The fifteenth-century Rood Screen of Partrishow

with machicolated gatehouse, courtyard, wooden galleries connected with allures corbelled out on both curtain-walls, and cantilevered roofs with quatrefoils and trefoils pierced in the main trusses.   Sir John Lloyd and the Brecknock Society have been largely responsible for this acquisition, as they have been responsible for much in this area, including the preservation of the medieval bridge at Aberbran and the institution of an annual service at Llansantffraed in honour of Vaughan.   Sixteen generations of Vaughans held Tretower until it was sold in 1783, and there are many curious references to both the family and the locality in the Star Chamber proceedings.   The original castle of Tretower also remains, a juliet or round tower *inside* a ruined Norman keep.

In the quilted country about Crickhowell is Gwernvale, a small mansion associated with Frederic William Rolfe, *soi-distant* Baron Corvo, the malignant genius of *Hadrian the Seventh*, and the birthplace in 1790 of Sir George Everest, surveyor-general of India, from whom Mount Everest was named.   Crickhowell itself is a somnolent market-town with a shingled church spire, a rarity in Wales, a fragment of a castle and the fifteenth-century gatehouse of a vanished mansion of the Herberts. The 'Crickhowell flannels' of Smollett's *Humphrey Clinker* are no more, but curfew still rings here and the long bridge over the Usk has a baker's dozen of arches.   Abergavenny and England are but six miles away, but we take the road to Llanbedr in the terraced and spurred Grwyne Fechan. Here the tiny church whets the appetite for what will be seen at Partrishow, for there is fifteenth-century glass and a good piece of contemporary diaper painting above the chancel arch, which served as a background to a rood and figures of St. Mary and St. John.   From here you must wriggle your way to Partrishow high in the Grwyne Fawr, another of the valleys with which these Black Mountains are trenched.   This is a place of some antiquity, manifest in the holy well of St. Issiu and the eleventh-century nave of a delicious church perched above a Tudor farmhouse. The church is a palimpsest, thirteenth-century chancel with double bell-cote, fourteenth-century timber roof in the century-earlier western chapel or cell, Tudor renovations, Elizabethan texts, Laudian altar-rails and excellent multi-coloured slate monuments designed and cut by local craftsmen in the eighteenth and early nineteenth centuries.   The focal point of all this is the magnificent rood-screen and loft, *temp.* Henry VII, of Irish oak richly carved with exuberant trailing foliage and vines issuing from the mouth of a Welsh dragon (54).   As the late Aymer Vallance pointed out, the tenacity of the Welsh people for their singing traditions may account for the preservation of rood-lofts in Wales when they all but vanished in England, and at Llanelieu, at the other end of the Gader Ridge, the hind part of the loft is pierced with quatrefoiled squints so that the singers could see the officiating priest below and would know when it was their turn to stand and lead the responses.

From Partrishow one must wriggle back to a road that follows the

Afon Honddu (not the Honddu that washes the back doorsteps of the Brecon cottages) to Llanthony. Since this is just in Monmouthshire we must be pedantic and ignore it. The valley, groves of beeches, sycamores and Spanish chestnuts above its slopes, is today almost as sparsely populated as it was when Giraldus accompanied Archbishop Baldwin to Llanthony Priory, but the community has dwindled from what it was a century ago. Nevertheless life goes on here much as ever in the lonely hillside sheep-farms, which cooperate on each other's shearing. The lonely lane runs beside the Honddu into the hamlet of Capel-y-ffin, and it is perhaps a matter of wonder that such a remote place should have become celebrated by virtue of its associations with two men of a very different calibre, Father Ignatius and Eric Gill. Much has been written about the Reverend Lester Lyne and his abortive attempt last century to found a community of Anglican monks. "Reverend Father, what are you?" asked the *New York Herald*. "As a monk you are a Roman Catholic, in orders you are an Episcopalian, in preaching you are a Calvinist, in exhortation a Methodist." He very confusingly called his place "Llanthony Abbey", which led to clashes with the Landors, owners of the original Priory, four miles away. Walter Savage Landor is another outstanding figure connected with this remote Border vale. A few Ignatius stories might be worth recording, though many are apocryphal. A prostitute did penance in a sheet at Elm Hill chapel, Norwich, a scold had to make public apology from the chancel steps, and Ignatius obligingly smashed up the high pews of St. Lawrence, Norwich, which the rector feared because of the feeling of his congregation to remove. No church in Oxford was open to him, and one evening he hired the Town Hall, which was crowded to the doors. At this meeting he announced that on the morrow he would conduct a special service for the lost in the Corn Exchange. It would have been interesting to see who patronised this latter meeting.[1]

The modern church of Ignatius yet stands, a mere shell, a Gothic ruin beside the cascaded stream, a John Piper painting. But the Puginesque monastic buildings nestling beneath the Fwddog Ridge were acquired by Eric Gill and other members of the Ditchling Guild and now form a delightful house in which the monks' partitioned cubicles are used as bedrooms, recalling the monastery-hotels of Sixt and Bad-Pfafers in Switzerland. The trials and joys of Gill's brief tenure, the search for the 'lost Bethlehem' and the Cobbett-like experiment to be self-supporting, may be read in his *Autobiography*, a self-searching document which has some affinity with *The Education of Henry Adams*. Gill practised what he

---

[1] A more remarkable, more authentic and perhaps more sincere renascence of English monastic life was that founded by Dom Aelred Carlyle early this century, culminating in the creation of the monastery on Caldey Island. Dom Aelred finally went to British Columbia, though I met him but recently on one of his rare visits to England. His Caldey community is now at Prinknash in the Cotswolds.

55   The Wye near Rhayader, Radnorshire

56  Llansantffraed, near Builth

57  Cascob, in Radnor Forest

RADNORSHIRE VILLAGE CHURCHES

preached, and the current turn of events may yet prove him to have been a prophet. Labour for Gill was a sacrament, a sacrament which the twentieth century has degraded. Life was rich and sensuous and good, but above it all was a divine purpose, and Gill saw beauty as Thomas Aquinas saw it, *id quod visum placet*.

A woman who had been housekeeper to the vicars of the box-like boundary-chapel for over thirty-six years told me much of the Spartan life in these hills. Until quite recent years many of the inhabitants were compelled to depend on Abergavenny or Hay for their provisions, and this in an area where winter is hard and floods frequent. Groceries would arrive weekly in a pair horse van, but now the Abergavenny bus comes up from Llanthony on market days. The remoteness of this valley may be further gauged from the fact that it is something of an unofficial bird-sanctuary, over ninety different birds having been identified. The tawny squirrels are indigenous, but are being driven into the hills by the grey species, which are foreigners and are destructive and carnivorous. There is a story that imported grey squirrels at the London Zoological Gardens escaped into Regent's Park, crossed the Chilterns and now infest the entire country. (A similar story about the red squirrel prevails in Canada.) Rhiw Wen at the head of the pass is a good point from which to ascend the stony heights of Waun Fach (2660 ft.) and Pen-y-Gader-fawr (2624 ft.) crowning the lofty plateau which begins where the dark pine-woods end. Or you may tramp under the lee of Hay Bluff and out of this delightful wilderness into Hay or Llanigon. Motorists (who come with safety only so far as Capel-y-ffin) must return whence they came, though adventurous honeymooners or sports car experts get through the bad track both ways.

It is as well to return to Tretower and reach Talgarth either through the Rhiangoll glen, below the shoulder of the humpbacked Mynydd Troed, or, preferably, via Bwlch and Llangorse. The best view of Llangorse Lake will be seen between Cathedine and Llangorse, of delicate beauty when seen in early evening with the distant peak of Pen-y-Fan as a drop-curtain, or when flooded with gold by sunlight. The bittern and the great crested grebe frequent the reedy land between here and Llangorse village, with its cradle-roofed church. Nearby is Treberyfydd, an Elizabethan house much cobbled by J. L. Pearson, with gardens laid by Nesfield. The road to Talgarth passes Trefecca, successor to the communal college for Calvinistic dissenters founded by Howel Harris in 1752 and based upon a system akin to that of the Moravians. Harris, with the collaboration of the Countess of Huntingdon, here erected an extravaganza in dubious contemporary taste, having Gothic embattle-ments, Corinthian capitals, and further touches of whimsy in topiary work. At Talgarth, where a stream flows through the village, there is little beyond the large church with fourteenth-century fortified tower and, near the bridge, a thirteenth-century tower which is a compromise between the local juliet and the Northumbrian 'bastel-house', but there is a group of interesting villages to be explored from here.   At Llanfilo the church (53) contains a rood-loft (60) with recent figures added and Llandefalle church has a coeval rood-screen minus the loft.   At Bronllys nearby, where the church has a detached fourteenth-century belfry, there are remains of a double screen such as may be seen to perfection at Llanelieu.   The main feature of Bronllys, however, is the castle or juliet which resembles that of Tretower, though this one has even more curious features.   Indeed, Victorian antiquaries have advanced the most exciting theories inferring that it is of Syriac workmanship, corresponding with Chardin's account of the Mingrelian castles of the east, and conceiving it to have been "an imitation of the work of the first stonemason after the Deluge, who settled in Britain".

The high road to Three Cocks skirts the fifteenth-century gatehouse of Porthamel and commands views of the long ridges of the Black Mountains (52) and of the bald hill discourteously known as Lord Hereford's Knob.   Beyond Three Cocks the Wye comes down from the north and circles north-eastwards.   The road following this eastern deflexion will take you to the folly-Gothic Maesllwch Castle, with the ancient Maes-y-ronnen chapel close by, the ancient border-town of Hay and Kilvert's Clyro, with a lovely hinterland in the Clyro and Llanbedr Hills, their lanes fragrant with wild roses and foxgloves.   The western road follows the silver Wye to Builth Wells, passing the Silurian Aberedw Rocks terraced above the valley and entering Aberedw, where lived Llewellyn, last of the Welsh princes, at the head of the wilfully pretty Edw glen.   The church contains a medieval rood-screen curiously surmounted by Stuart balustrading.   Builth, though largely Georgian, need not detain you, but you must follow the Yrfon valley to Llanwrtyd Wells for the sake of old Llanwrtyd, which lies a mile farther up the valley at the foot of Garn Dwad, and for the walk from there to Abergwesyn.   From a point near the latter, Tregaron may be gained by the overland track still used by drovers and their flocks, who take two days and one night on the journey from Tregaron to Brecon market.

The treeless Radnor Forest, a high moorland culminating in Great Rhos, stretches north-eastward from Builth.   Though there is but barren pasturage, sheep-farming thrives by dint of hard work, and it is as sheep-country that we think of it, as David Cox thought of it, for he painted and drew innumerable studies of Welsh shepherds and cattle, many of them in Radnorshire.   It is a county with some English characteristics, for it is neighboured by both Hereford and Shropshire, from which the timber-framed tradition overflows.   Kilvert has caught the spirit of this countryside and framed it for ever in the pages of his *Diary*.   One remembers his warm phrase, "the beautiful courtesy of Radnorshire", as one tramps the villages of the 'Forest' and of the upper Teme.   One must go to Georgian Presteigne on the Lugg to dine in the Radnorshire Arms and see the Jerusalem tapestry in the church; to New Radnor, where there are snowdrops in the churchyard and where the old parsonage was an inn only last century; to Knighton for Pilleth Court, with its Elizabethan panelling and carving, Knill Court, Elizabethan with a medieval nucleus, and The Rodd, a manor-house with Jacobean enriched ceilings and overmantels. The remote churches of this area provide a constant delight: Cascob with its timbered belfry (57), Beguildy, Cefn-Llys, Llandegley with its seven-fold doorway (and here too is an eighteenth-century Quaker chapel with golden thatch on sunlit stone), Old Radnor, Llanbister and Llananno in the valley of the Ithon. All these contain rood-screens or lofts or both, and Llananno has an iconographical parapet and some exquisite tabernacle work. And from Llananno a glen cuts across to the Clywedog valley and the lonely outpost of Abbey Cwmhir, a daughter house of Cistercian Whitland. The twelfth-century ruins are negligible, consisting only of a few foundations. There are a few mildly stormy chapters in its history, mainly occasioned by rebellious *conversi* or lay-brethren, who once stole their abbot's horses in revenge for his prohibiting beer, and who were compelled to do penance at Clairvaux.

We are pledged to follow the Wye yet farther, from Builth via Newbridge, with its horse-fairs, and Disserth church, with Jacobean pews and pulpit, to Rhayader, where a detour must be made to the valleys of the Elan and its tributary the Claerwen. Much of this area has been dammed to provide water for Birmingham, and the reservoirs are not entirely lacking in character (45), the great dam of Caban Coch bestriding the valley like an enraged giant. Shelley would find it vastly different from the days when he lived with the gentle Harriet in Nantgwyllt, now below the water. I have tramped across country from here to Devil's Bridge, but can recommend such a walk only to hermits and philosophers. Therefore you will probably return to Rhayader (66) and continue to Llangurig, a pretty village in the foothills of Plynlimon. The Wye has become a chattering infant and you may track it to its cradle. Northward a sister river, the Severn, has also become a turbulent mountain stream, but at Llanidloes this youngster is already an infant prodigy. The Montgomery night is still and crystal clear, and the twilight hours may be beguiled by a novel by Geraint Goodwin or Eiluned Lewis, both delineators of this aromatic countryside.

NOTE: The author apologises for what he considers to be niggardly treatment of the area covered by the latter part of this chapter. He pleads restricted space, and the fact that this area has been generously dealt with by topographers. See especially *Welsh Border Country*, by Thoresby Jones.

CHAPTER

# VIII

## MONTGOMERY AND THE MOORLANDS
## VALE OF MEIFOD    CEIRIOG VALLEY
## THE BERWYN MOUNTAINS

LLANIDLOES, originally cross-shaped, is bridged over both Severn and Clywedog and is yet noted for mutton and flannel. The buildings were formerly timber-framed in the idiom of the surviving Market House with its curfew bell, and even the tower of the church (which contains an excellent thirteenth-century arcade with clustered piers and palm-leaved capitals, also a richly figured hammer-beam roof ) has a wooden belfry. An exploration of this area will reveal the most highly perfected technique of timber-framed building in Wales. In the area of Trefeglwys are several excellent examples, of which the best are Talgarth, with angle-posts and braces and dormers, and Rhyd-y-carw, with a gabled porch-wing and stone gable-ends with projecting chimneys. At Caersws is Maes-mawr, with quadrant studding in the gabled porch-wing (and Georgian sashes) and a curious interior in which hall, parlour and staircases are grouped about a central chimney. The boarded treatment may be seen in cottages and farmhouses on the moorlands between here and Machynlleth. A more localised characteristic is the laying of pitched and patterned cobbled floors such as may be seen in houses about Llanwynog and the lonely moorland village of Carno, where descendants of Richard Wilson, the landscape painter, kept the Merchant of Aleppo Inn until a few years ago. And at Llanwnog the church has a fifteenth-century rood-loft with beautiful Gothic traceried and pierced panels (59).

The Severn has already forgotten its humble birth and swells itself with a cocksure pride as it flows through moorland country with low wooded hills to Newtown (65). The town belies its name, though in truth the melancholy old houses which survive, the best of which is the thatched and timbered Chequers Inn, are all but shouldered out by the red-brick flannel factories and warehouses, the tanneries and malt-houses, the Victorian Town Hall and Cloth Hall. A Victorian church supersedes the old parish church, which in spite of some excellent characteristics has been allowed to fall into ruin. Here you may pay your devoirs to Robert Owen, first of the dynasty of disillusioned pioneers of Socialism,

58   In Montgomery Parish Church

59   At Llanwnog, Montgomeryshire

**FIFTEENTH-CENTURY ROOD SCREENS**

60  Llanfilo Church, Brecknockshire:
    an un-restored Interior

61 Llanegryn Church, Merionethshire:
   a detail of the fifteenth-
   century Rood Screen

and the Owen Memorial Museum occupies part of a building on the site of his birthplace. Nor must we forget Sir John Pryse, a former squire of Newtown Hall, who might have stepped from the pages of Edgar Allen Poe, for he married three times, keeping the bodies of the first two wives in an embalmed state, placing them one on each side of his bed and introducing a third wife to keep him company; the last wife, however, would have none of it and refused to act as sleeping-partner until her predecessors had been removed. But we cannot leave Newtown without some record of the Gregynog Press, founded in 1921, with its brilliant team of artists and designers, which, almost alone in this country, presents a form of community handicraft which William Morris revived, and which a few such as C. R. Ashbee continued.

Southward of the road to Montgomery stretch the desolate Kerry Hills (so-called since the Herberts held estates in County Kerry) prolonged eastward by the Clun Forest. The late Geraint Goodwin, a highly sensitive artist, has framed the rich vital peasant life of these hills as securely as a fly caught in amber. Rarely writing more than three hundred words a day, with the spectre of tuberculosis ever at hand, the novelist chose to live in this remote country rather than in the limelight of fashionable Bloomsbury. He scored an early success with *Conversations with George Moore*, but at the age of thirty he began all over again and wrote *The White Farm, The Heyday in the Blood* and others. He was dead at thirty-eight.

Montgomery itself (63) is entirely charming from the moment one enters it below the rocky height, an outcrop of the long Kerry Hills, crowned with the shattered towers of a thirteenth-century castle. This was the early home of Edward, Lord Herbert of Chirbury and of his brother, George Herbert. Edward, who was celebrated alike for chivalry, scholarship and deism, was the author of the rollicking autobiography, *De Veritate*, probably the earliest metaphysical treatise written by an Englishman (or Welshman), and such minor works as a biography of Henry the Eighth. He was a belligerent diplomat frequently involved in duels, but appears to have been an engaging fellow, and Saintsbury may have been rather severe in his verdict: ". . . not a very bad poet . . . a very great coxcomb, and a hero chiefly by his own report." But George Herbert was the real genius of the family, as he was yet another of the seventeenth-century religious poets with which Wales has enriched English literature. His affinities with Vaughan are obvious, for he had a touch of that Silurism which seems to be endemic in literary Marchers (even the late Arthur Machen did not escape it).

The plan of the little town remains largely as it was mapped by Speed in the seventeenth century, and there is little or no modern fabric to spoil the picture, though there is a large Classical rusticated gatehouse of 1866 fronting the earlier gaol. The latter is a ruined shell of which the windows yet retain their iron grilles, now pranked with the red valerian which the natives call 'pretty Betty'. The market square is dominated by the late Georgian Guildhall, rather prudish, with arched treatment, wooden pediment and cupola, and the cobbled pavements of converging streets are lined with reticent old houses. One attractive house of colour-washed brick has a curious gable and is itself chaperoned by an elderly matron of the same family. Nearby are two good Regency shop-fronts, and elsewhere the houses are timber-framed with plaster or stone or brick, all roofed with mossy slats and often featuring 'Gothick' casements. All these houses seem to surge upward to the magpie-coloured Dragon Inn, with its main and subsidiary gables, and here, where the houses end and the woods begin, is a stone fountain flourishing an armorial panel and wrought-iron lamp bracket. It is a delightful spot, the powder-blue wood smoke from the cottages pirouetting against the sage-green wooded hill. This landscape is enhanced when seen across the huddle of roofs from the churchyard, a belvedere on the far side of the square. Within the church are more treasures, a fifteenth-century double rood-screen, the loft having ogee arches and crocketed finials upon the parapet, with Elizabethan carved and voluted oak gates in the centre, and a glittering canopied monument to Richard Herbert, its Corinthian shafts framing a semi-circular recess and supporting a cornice with gilded arabesques. On the edge of the town are Ffridd Faldwyn, the huge rampart of a Late Iron Age settlement, and the Gaer, a Roman camp, while Offa's Dyke runs through Lymore Park, where it remains the boundary between England and Wales. Lymore Hall, an excellent late example, 1675, of the timber-framed technique, was recently demolished.

Berriew, bridged over the rock-bedded Rhiw, is entirely a black-and-white village (62) and probably presents the largest ensemble of timber-framed houses in Wales, but its church with cone-capped tower is Victorian and serves as a warning that the restorers have been at work in the area. In Powys Castle, set in a fine park of Gargantuan oaks and firs, we have more tangible proof of this, for while this red sandstone mansion seems, from a respectable distance, a convincing enough medieval castle (for it has embattled drum-towers), we shall find the heavy hand of Smirke in some weak neo-Gothic additions to what was virtually a Jacobean rebuilding. Internally there is a rich assortment: a few thirteenth-century walls, a sixteenth-century gallery, a painted staircase of 1705, a state-bedroom as prepared for Charles I and curiosities brought from India by Robert Clive (to whose family the estate descended from the Herberts). But the banqueting-hall of Sir Walter Scott's *The Betrothed*, the "long, low hall, built of rough wood lined with shingles", has long gone. A Herbert of 1688 fled the country with James II and was outlawed, whereupon William III gave the castle to one of his Dutch satellites; but the Herberts, more fortunate than most Jacobites, recovered it thirty years later. The park of Powys in June is sheer joy, the sunlight weaving the branches of wrestling trees into filigree, the swathed warm,

62   The Village of Berriew, Montgomeryshire

63   Montgomery Town

glistening grass, the plain-chant of bees. And in the terraced gardens, which Pennant declared to be "in imitation of the wretched taste of St. Germains-en-Laye", the lead figures of shepherds and shepherdesses above the orangery almost dance. We must not forget, however, that 'Capability' Brown also had a hand here.

In Welshpool the church was completely cobbled by Street (who also restored Montgomery church and designed a new one at Llandulas), and is remarkable for its huge porches and distorted ground-plan. Yet Welshpool, ostensibly English, is not without character. It has early malt-houses and the novelty of a light railway running through the town and transporting sheep and minerals to and from Llanfair Caereinion. There are a number of old inns, such as the former Cross Keys, with its Royalist inscription invoking a curse upon Cromwell; the fifteenth-century Prentice Traders' tea-shop, with quadrant studding and a lower storey divided into bays with curved braces forming arches; and the Mermaid, attractively restored; while the former Castle Inn, now the post office, retains a long sweep of Georgian sashes. Late Georgian houses predominate; there is a neat stuccoed bank of 1816 and a coeval cottage-terrace with its upper storey jettied over a wooden colonnade. At the Cross is a house to which all those blessed with the patronymic of Jones should come in pilgrimmage, for here in the seventeenth century lived Anne and Gilbert Jones, whose ancestor, Roger Jones (*temp.* Edward I), was the first of the clan. This house later became the home of Robert Owen, a saddler, to whose son we (or some of us) have already paid homage at Newtown.

Llanfair Caereinion on the road to Dinas Mawddwy is a picturesque grey little town jumbled upon a bank of the Einion, and here again the church is largely Victorian, though it embodies a good thirteenth-century doorway with clustered shafts and 'birds-beak' mouldings on abaci and capitals. The Vale of Meifod is conveniently entered from here, but one should climb a hill-track near its mouth in quest of the lonely church of Llangyniew, which has some curious features and fragments of screen tracery. This is rich, placid country. A plantation of larch crawls like a giant caterpillar along the crest of the hills. Early morning mists cut off the hill-tops and leaves them hanging in mid-air. Soon we strike the imperceptibly moving Vyrnwy, for these moorlands sloping down from the Berwyns are trenched by an august hierarchy of streams, the Banwy, Ceiriog, Tanat, Carno and Vyrnwy. Farther northward the elongated white Regency house of Penylan nestles below the high cone of Bronieth, while immediately westward rise the craggy heights of Dyffryn. Eastward there are glimpses of the triune peaks of the startling and quite fantastic Breiddens, though not seen to good advantage from here. In Meifod the timber-frame tradition seems already lost, for the charming village is brick and stone built. The cottages have Georgian fronts, and the King's Head Inn has pediment, Palladian window and gated staircase.

The church has been tampered with, but retains a thirteenth-century tower and is the first we have yet encountered that approaches in plan the twin-naved churches of nearby Denbighshire; there were formerly two, possibly three, churches in the circular churchyard (cf. Penmachno in Caernarvon). Meifod was celebrated in early Welsh poetry and was a *maifod* or summer residence of the princes of Powys; Mathrafal farmhouse nearby claims to occupy the actual site. We pick up the Vyrnwy again and reach Llansantffraed yn Mechain, an anglers' village with a fourteenth-century church altered three centuries later, having a Jacobean window and timbered porch and steeple. Llanfechain on the Cain stream also has Jacobean additions, notably an inscribed pulpit, and contains among other things a Georgian wrought-iron chandelier. We shall see that Jacobean activity in the churches of northern Wales is very marked.

Llanfyllin lies amid steep, wooded hills in the valley of the Cain, a tributary of the Vyrnwy. Here the timber-frame to which we are so accustomed in this area is restored, though the buildings are invariably refronted with later brickwork. The Wynnstay Arms has a late Georgian façade and 'Gothick' glazing in the curious bar, but its well-staircase, with carved newels and pendants, is Jacobean. This was one of the inns which served the potent ale said to fill Llanfyllin with young widows. The town is many-hued and has some pleasing features, an imposing Regency workhouse, houses with moulded segments to the windows, a neat house of 1737 with original sashes, quoins and six-fielded-panelled door with pedimented weather-hood on scrolled modillion brackets, and, nearby, frowning cream-washed villas in the Tudor Gothic of *c.* 1850. The red-brick parish church is a frigid conventicle of the eighteenth century, somewhat relieved by stone doorcases in bolection mouldings, the lintels inscribed in Latin, and neo-Norman windows as ugly as the Victorians could make them. Nearby is a plain brick house of perhaps *c.* 1800 which contains a most interesting relic in the form of full-length frescoes on the plaster walls of a bedroom, the work of a Napoleonic prisoner-of-war. These murals portray fantastic rock scenery in vivid colours, with purples and blues predominating. Of crude execution and slightly savouring of the early Impressionists, they display some originality, though the *motif* is rather repetitive. They may represent the coast of Normandy or possibly some tarn scenery in the Pyrenees; certainly there is a hint of the south in the Corinthian temple; but it is pictorial hyperbole and is probably the by-product of dreams inspired by nostalgia and home-sickness. Within living memory a Frenchman arrived in Llanfyllin and declared that the work was that of his grandfather.

North of Llanfyllin lies the verdant valley of the Tanat, and just beyond is Llangedwyn Hall, a large, rambling house, multi-gabled and dormered, with Georgian sashes, lying at the end of an avenue of lines fronted by great palisades. This was the home of that Charles Williams-Wynn who was the brother of the baronet of Wynnstay and who brought his

old school-fellow Robert Southey (with Bishop Heber) to taste the
delights of this countryside. Nearby, beyond Pont Sycharth, is the site
of Sycharth, a residence of Owen Glyndowr. This was the Welshman
who raised the standard of revolt against all English rule, a man whom
Shakespeare (in *Henry the Fourth*) limned as one who was "not in the
roll of common men". It has now become rather fashionable to doubt
his integrity. Certainly there is much evidence of hypocrisy and selfish
ambition, of the needless excesses which he (or his mobs) committed in
the cause of Wales, and of the misery which he often brought upon his
own people. But there is, too, much evidence of his statesmanship, in
his petition for a national university and in his remarkable conclaves or
early parliaments, and the following (perhaps true) parable provides an
apt epitaph. The abbot of Valle Crucis was walking on the Berwyns
early one morning when he encountered Glyndowr, now old, overthrown
and dejected. "Sir Abbot," remarked Glyndowr as he rose to meet
him, "you have risen too early." "No," the abbot replied, "it is you
who have risen too early—by a hundred years." The Tanat valley may
be followed to Llangynog, but the Ceiriog valley and the hinterland of
the Berwyns lie northwards through an area rich in fifteenth- and sixteenth-century cottages, through Llansilin, where lies Huw Morris, the
Royalist satirical poet, from where a road branches off to Llanarmon-
Duffryn-Ceiriog. Westward stretch the bald, lofty ridges between
Cader Fronwen and Moel Sych. The 'merlin', or Welsh mountain-pony
(the 'pygmean steed' of Dyer, the poet), ranges these high hills until it
is three years old, when it is brought down for sale at Llanfyllin market.

Llanarmon sits at the foot of Mynydd Tarw, and from it a tantalising
road runs southward for a short distance to end abruptly in mid-country.
There is little here but the old smithy where the farrier is at work and
the gabled Old West Arms, a cosy inn. All about are the tilted fields,
with Cader Fronwen looming nearer. From Llanarmon the road follows
the deep valley of the sparkling Ceiriog all the way to Chirk. Beyond
the tranquil hamlets of Tregeiriog and Pandy is Llansantffraed-Glyn-
Ceiriog, its village community quarrying this serene country, though not,
as yet, obtrusively. There is a granite memorial to John Ceiriog Hughes,
the station-master poet beloved of Borrow, and the village institute com-
memorates more than forty distinguished Welshmen, claiming as one
of them Thomas Jefferson, the American statesman. The old house of
Dolywern stands aloof, and beyond Pontfaen, with its trout-hatchery, we
skirt the deer park of Chirk Castle. The castle (80, 102) stands some two
miles beyond the entrance-gates, which are highly festive in design, of
scrolled and gilded early-eighteenth-century wrought-iron, the work of
the Davies brothers of Bersham. John and Robert Davies worked with
both Jean Tijou and Robert Bakewell on more than one occasion, and
their work is among the finest of the period. We shall encounter
it again at Ruthin, Mold, Emral Hall and Erdig, while immediately

outside our area it may be seen at Eaton Hall near Chester.   The dark red castle is Edwardian, rectangular with corner drums, but the details are largely of the seventeenth century, and the courtyard with its mullioned fenestration resembles a college quad.   The Victorian additions, including a low, embattled corridor around two sides of the courtyard and some internal decoration, are the work of Augustus Welby Pugin, who attempted to restore to the muddled architectural forms of the nineteenth century the sanity and order of the thirteenth.   Pugin's spirit belonged to a medieval cloister but his flesh was rooted in the new industrial England of the early Victorians, and he lived in what (as a Catholic) he must have regarded as Purgatory.   We shall encounter his work only once more in Wales, at Pantasaph in Flint, though he designed a girls' school at Chirk for the owner of the castle; the school is not remarkable, though its south elevation is plausible and characteristic.   The village itself lies on the Denbighshire bank of the Ceiriog.   There are yew-trees in its churchyard, and the church contains a good fifteenth-century roof, a Georgian pulpit and monuments to the Myddletons, of which that to a Lady Middleton appears to have been designed by John Bushnell.

From Chirk you may be straightway tempted to enter the Vale of Llangollen, but this is best approached from the north-west, and since the Berwyns yet hold us in thrall it is better to return to Llansilin and branch off, crossing the Iwrch, to Llanrhaiadr-ym-Mochnant, which has some old glass in the church.   From here the narrow glen of the Rhaiadr dividing Montgomeryshire from Denbighshire, runs below Moel Sych, and at its head is the Pistyll Rhaiadr, the cascaded fall of the Afon Disgynfa, which is precipitated over a sheer cliff and thence through a natural arch into a deep cauldron.   This is perhaps the finest waterfall in Wales, and it has moved many topographers to use extravagant metaphors. Above the lonely farmhouse is the rock-bound tarn of Llyn Llyncaws, from whence the summit of Moel Sych may be gained.   Re-crossing the Tanat one comes to the delightful hamlet of Penybont Fawr, from which a mountainous road leads via Hirnant and the model village of Llanwddyn to Lake Vyrnwy.   This is an artificial reservoir created to supply water for Liverpool, but the landscape lacks the wild grandeur of the Elan valley, with its chain of lakes.   The road from here to Bala through the Hirnant valley, however, is one of the grandest mountain roads in Wales, though tricky for vehicles, and Bala is best reached via Llangynog.   Llangynog has a highly picturesque setting at the confluence of the Tanat and the Eiarth, above which rises the great mass of Craig Rhiwarth.   Harps were formerly made here, and latterly there was much granite-quarrying and lead-mining in the district, but these industries have died out.   The village is stone-built and austere, but we have left the Marches behind us, for this community is thoroughly Welsh.   Opposite the inn of Queen Anne's reign, with its scrolled ironwork sign, is the way through the scarped mountain valley of the Pennant, brocaded with wild

65　The Sheep Fair at Newtown, Montgomeryshire

66　A Harvest Scene near Rhayader, Radnorshire

67, 68   From the air (*above*) and
the Staircase (*c.* 1660) (*left*)

POWIS CASTLE,
MONTGOMERYSHIRE

roses in June. And in the hamlet of Pennant Melangell is a pleasant native church, with a primitive dovecote-like tower, a fifteenth-century rood-screen, some medieval effigies and an eighteenth-century wooden candelabrum which has its twin at Rhug. A beam of the loft now on a western gallery is enriched with mutilated carvings illustrating the seventh-century legend of St. Monacella (Melangell), who defied a frustrated, snarling pack of hounds and gave a fugitive hare refuge beneath her robe, and who henceforth became the patron-saint of hares, 'St. Monacella's lambs' as they became known in the district. The churchyard contains the remains of a cock pit. The road peters out and there are but sheep tracks over the moorlands.

Beyond Llangynog the road climbs along the eastern flank of the broad, deep Eiarth valley, passing the great crags of Craig-y-Castell and Craig Rhiwarth and proceeding along an unfenced road over the face of a precipitous slope. At the Milltir Gerrig Pass (sometimes known as the Berwyn Pass) one enters Merioneth. From the summit the moorlands and mountains open out, and in the distance, beyond the Bala 'cleft', lies Arenig Fawr, with the Clwydian range northward. Descending the northern slope one finds the Afon Calettwr bubbling in capricious mood along its rocky bed and hanging these hills with milky cascades. Though the farmhouses are not far away, there is little sign of human activity here, only sheep, a few goats and occasionally a cock pheasant. Where the stream is bridged you may leave the Bala road for Llandderfel in the Dee Valley, a village of whitewashed stone cottages holding itself aloof from the high road. The church is of good Perpendicular work and has a rood-screen of c. 1500 and some good tracery and glass in the east window. Two singular medieval relics are preserved here, the wooden image of a horse (looking curiously like a deer) and the remains of an annuleted pole. The first is reputed to be a fragment of an equestrian figure of St. Derfel, and the second, less plausibly, the staff of the saint. The figure of the saint which surmounted the horse was removed in the holocaust of the Reformation and added to the sacrificial pile that consumed poor Friar Forest, Catherine of Aragon's confessor, at Smithfield.[1] Llandderfel has more odd history, for Gaynor Hughes, one of the 'fasting girls' of eighteenth-century Wales, here lived without real food for eight years, dying aged thirty-five in 1786. Earlier, temp. Charles II, a number of Llandderfel Quakers emigrated to Philadelphia.

Bala lies southward along the Dee valley (76), but I prefer to return to the Llangynog road and approach it from the east. This pretext will take us, with a little deviation, to the hamlet of Rhos-y-gwaliau, clustered about a rippling, boulder-strewn stream, just below Plas Rhiwaedog, a melancholy and fallen manor-house of 1644 with gabled gatehouse, fore-court and central porch-wing, its staircase now groaning beneath the

[1] I believe that the brass tablet affixed to the original relic yet survives in the British Museum.

9**

weight of youth-hostellers.   This is in the purlieus of the wild Hirnant valley, a remote area in which people yet hang a wand of hazel above the fireplace in order to ward off witches and evil spirits.   And as we drop down into Bala we find ourselves emulating a Victorian Dean of Chester who was fond of applying the cliché 'Alpine' to these hills.

# IX

## BALA   THE DYFI VALLEY   DOLGELLEY AND THE MAWDDACH ESTUARY   THE MERIONETH COAST   THE VALE OF FFESTINIOG

THE four seasons mould a country as they mould a character, and acquaintance with this area in one particular season of the year is obviously inadequate. One must see it, for example, at the turn of the leaf when the high hills are hung with faded tapestry. I have seen Bala Lake flooded with summer gold, but I have seen it too in mid-winter, bathed in purplish mist, the foothills white with hoar frost and a glimmer of sun gilding the uplands. Beyond rise the mountains, Arenig Fawr, Cader Idris and the Arans. The lake is celebrated for its white-scaled fish, the gwyniad, which a former Lord Lyttleton declared "to more than rival in flavour the lips of the fair maids of Bala". (Lyttleton was not the only one to go a-philandering in Bala; de Quincey and others are suspect.) The social activities of the town are rather different from what they were in the eighteenth and early nineteenth centuries, when all the women knitted worsted stockings, gloves and 'neck-wrappers', in winter holding knitting assemblies at one and another's houses and in summer sitting upon the *tomen*, an early earthwork, still knitting, like Dickens' Madame Defarge.

The wide, tree-planted high street of Bala is almost deserted at all times save for Saturday evenings, when the inns overflow and groups of stocky men ruminate outside the Town Hall. Nearby is Goscombe John's bronze statue of Thomas Ellis, a local man of farming stock who went up to Oxford at a time when Arnold Toynbee was lecturing at Balliol. Ellis was influenced by the tenets of Mazzini in matters of politics and nationalism, became Member of Parliament for Merioneth and released that county from a tenebrous feudalism. Another of Bala's celebrities, Thomas Charles, who has been called the Wesley of Wales, has his statue here, and the neo-Gothic Theological College, formerly Calvinistic, was one of the fruits of his teaching. Borrow's breakfast at the White Lion now seems apocalyptic, but this inn remains an excellent hostelry. In the park of Plas Rhiwlas the Treweryn rushes and tumbles in cascades to meet the Dee, and it is not surprising to find a 'Gothick' mansion in such a landscape. Rhiwlas is an embattled house with side and central towers, quatrefoiled windows and plaster vaults. It belongs to a group of houses which includes Brynkenalt, near Chirk, Halkin Castle and Hawarden Castle, and a rain-water-head dated 1809 brings it into the very year in which Hawarden was built.

Llanuwchllyn, happily set between lake, moorland and mountain, is a resort of contemplative, poker-faced anglers, and its rebuilt church contains a curious portable wooden baptistery, a Victorian relic of that Welsh ardour for total immersion. The Tudor house of Caer Gai stands within what may have been a Roman enclosure and is traditionally the site of the home of Cynyr, the Ector of the *Morte d'Arthur*. The road to Dolgelley ascends the Dyfrdwy and drops down into the valley of the Wnion, a wild region overshadowed by Aran Benllyn. Ahead lie Cader Idris and the steep face of Tyrau-Mawr. But we prefer to leave Llanuwchllyn by the Bwlch y Groes, one of the wildest and steepest mountain roads in Britain, climbing Cwm Cynllwyd above the boulder-strewn Twrch to the summit at the head of the Rhiwlech glen. Immediately westward are the dark peaks, gleaming with white quartz, of the twin Arans. The glen descends into an amphitheatre of mountain slopes down which pour numerous little *afons*. The hamlet of Llanymawddwy has not even the solace of an inn, and we suspect it to cling tenaciously to its traditions, for in the yew-screened church males and females are yet segregated, as they are in Calvinist communities on the Continent. The Dyfi (or Dovey) flows in from the west and the valley is now partly wooded, and in the vicinity of Abercowarch are some pretty streams and waterfalls.

Dinas Mawddwy sprawls along a ledge above the Dyfi and the Cerist, a grey, prosaic enough slate-quarrying village. But what a setting! I know of few villages hemmed in by such mountains hung with rejuvenated plantations of emerald-green larches. The slate industry has declined, and there is a note of abandonment which is enhanced by the broken campanile tower of the ruined Victorian manor-house, gabled and mullioned like a seventeenth-century *plas*, its garden a wilderness of tangled rhododendrons. But everything is dwarfed by the mountain masses on every side. In Pennant's time there was a mayor (he was the local blacksmith), and almost a century ago mad John Mytton, the Shropshire eccentric, was squire. The defiles of Dinas look even more glorious from the hamlet of Mallwyd, itself an Arcady where the king-fisher dives swiftly into the river, which here carves its way through the rock. The fishing inn, slate-hung without, part timber-framed within, is a cosy snuggery primed with antiques, glistening brass, fishing-rods, log-fires and rooms with a view. The fulling-mill of Cotman's water-colour has gone, but there are pleasant cottages, an old bridge and an intriguing church in a circular churchyard planted with venerable yews. I have been here at Christmas (and this is a land of Christmas-trees) when

69   The Ganllwyd Valley, Merionethshire

70 A Street in Harlech, Merionethshire

71 The Court house, Dolgelley, Merionethshire

WELSH VERNACULAR

all the cottage parlours have been filled with song, families gathered together, a son from the University at Aberystwyth, a daughter from a London hospital, another son from an office in the cold drab north of England, for a Welsh homecoming is a time of joy.  The church is partly thirteenth-century, but has seventeenth-century barrel-roofed chancel, wooden belfry tower and timbered south porch, all added by Dr. John Davies, who defied the rubric decreed by Archbishop Laud and insisted upon the central altar of ancient usage.  Davies appears to have been a talented martinet; as a grammarian he raised the level of the Welsh language of his day (probably then as crude and undeveloped as the English of Chaucer's time) and wrote a Welsh-Latin dictionary, while his revised version of the Scriptures now lies on every lectern of the Established Church in Wales.  In addition to the Church alterations, he built a number of bridges over the Dyfi and also the present rectory, since altered.

The Dyfi valley to Machynlleth presents a landscape which Richard Wilson knew intimately, and which he must have loved, and to see it at almost any time of the year is to be confounded by the anaemia of English painting.  Rarely does one see such colours, even under a mid-winter's sun, bronze, russets, olives, greens of every hue, mauve, the ever-changing light and shade a constant delight.  The hamlet of Aberhangel fits snugly into the valley with something of a Latin or southern *comble*, for one enters it beneath an archway through which one must return, the mountain closing down abruptly behind the village.  Farther down the valley remote-looking farmsteads stud the lower slopes of the hills, on which small forests are neatly spread like carpets.  In the rectory of Penegoes was born one who has had a major influence on British landscape-painting.  The son of a clergyman, Richard Wilson was born in the year of Queen Anne's death; after a visit to Italy he abandoned portraiture for landscapes and was later influenced by the Classical traditions of Claude and Poussin, though he remained essentially a Romantic.

Machynlleth is inoffensive but unexciting, its Victorian clock-tower dominating the humble square, in the purlieus of which are a Borrovian inn and a smithy with stone-studded horseshoe entrance.  Parliament House is reputed to have been a residence of Glyndowr, who was here crowned Prince of Wales in 1402, and the present building, picturesquely cobbled up in medieval idiom, retains an arched gatehouse and some original features.  Almost opposite is the tertian-Gothic lodge of the *plas*, an uninteresting mansion lately given by the Marquess of Londonderry to the town (he was presented with a gift of four volumes, poems of George Herbert, Henry Vaughan, W. H. Davies and Walter de la Mare, all printed by the Gregynog Press and bound in leather at the National Library of Wales—a not unequal exchange).  The environs of the town are worthy of more attention.  There is the sweet valley of the Afon Dulas, which presently forks out into numerous streams which lose themselves in the moorlands, and there is the more majestic Llyfnant valley, which runs from the lower Dyfi. The road through Pennal, with a picturesque Georgian church and cornfields covering the site of a Roman station, eventually returns to the Dovey estuary and reaches Aberdovey, fringed with golden sands.

This small watering-place, with its homely Wesleyan chapel in the square, is of some antiquity, and Llewelyn's convening of Welsh princes here in 1216 was virtually the first Welsh parliament. Its flats and hards have known days of craftsmanship and pride, for during the last century there were here busy ship-building yards, and schooners, sloops and brigs left their slips to transport the riches of the lead-mines and the slate of the Corris mountain. Between 1840–80 some eighty vessels were built on the river, most of them in the Aberdovey yards. Here and there one encounters old prints of the copper-bottomed *Mervinia*, the brig *Alice* in full rig, and the *Dovey Belle*, last of the old dynasty. Slightly earlier vessels of these types may be seen in aquatints by William Daniell (himself of Welsh extraction), and it is worthy of record that in the eighteenth century the construction of these Aberdovey ships was influenced by Dutch models, a vogue which came over here after the Restoration. The registers of Towyn church nearby are crowded with the names of shipwrights and mariners, and in the churchyard a host of seamen lie beneath the slate tombstones, on which is sometimes inscribed, very simply, *morwr* or sailor. Towyn is excelled by Aberdovey in that the latter has a mountain for background. Yet Towyn has its own configuration of marsh-lands and distant hills and is perhaps the richer in interest. Its church, spoiled by modern solecisms, has an early-Norman nave with rude cylindrical piers, primitively whitewashed, some quatrefoils pierced above the main roof-trusses, and the curious elongated St. Cadfan's stone, *c.* 650, with the earliest known example of a Welsh inscription. The domestic architecture of the area is also of interest, particularly Dolau Gwyn, an early-seventeenth-century mansion with stepped gables and a beautifully enriched and panelled plaster ceiling, and Ynysmaen-gwyn, one of the very few pure mid-eighteenth-century designs in Wales (cf. Plas Gwyn in Anglesey), of three bays, with central pediment, quoins and pedimented doorcase.

At Llanegryn, beyond the marshes of the Dysynni, the little church contains a magnificent late-fourteenth-century rood-screen and loft, the traceried and pierced panels, all different, of the bressummer a study in ingenious and exuberant design. The coastal route to Dolgelley has obvious charms, but the rough road through the wooded Dysynni valley to Tal-y-Llyn shows the pattern of the country to greater advantage. The hamlet of Tal-y-Llyn, with a church of *c.* 1600, its chancel roof painted with red and white roses, is set at the end of the lake, which is deeply hollowed and surrounded by the sombre blueish precipices of Cader Idris (74). Seen from the head of the pass it is dramatic. The *direct* ascent of Cader may be made from here, though it is not the easiest, and while much of this mountain is a dreary waste of basaltic rock it has character and diversity enough, and its seven-pronged summit is a grand belvedere. The head of the pass opens on to the Machynlleth-Dolgelley road in the vicinity of slaty Corris, a road which is apt to play tricks upon the unwary traveller, for one of the mountains moves on clay during the wet season, and at Ffidd Gate a detour of eight miles must sometimes be made because of the frequently flooded Dyfi, a river tidal from Dolgelynen.

Dolgelley (77) is one of the bleakest of Welsh towns, grey-walled and slate-roofed, and a stranger on a Sunday in mid-winter may invoke alliterative curses upon a puritanical regime which abruptly closes all communications and amenities. Yet he may with a little imagination find much to intrigue him in the narrow alleys, hemmed with old cottages with stone gabled dormers and mellowed slats, and hearing an angelic choir in the Bethel chapel he may (having never entered such a conventicle) be as fascinated as I have been when coming suddenly upon the singing of invisible nuns in a remote village of Majorca. For nothing could be further removed from the English idiom than this old town, which until recently relied upon currying and tanning and weaving the coarse woollen cloth known as 'Welsh webs'. Little remains of yet another Parliament House in which Glyndowr held a conclave in 1404, signing his alliance with Charles VI of France in the following year, but the modest almshouses are of the early seventeenth century. We have as yet seen few almshouses in Wales, for there was never (until the present benighted century) that problem of poverty that existed in England, the majority of thrifty, hard-working smallholders being self-supporting, and even at the Reformation there were no masses of people thrown upon the charity of the State, as there were in England. There is a Georgian hint of sobriety in the box-dormers of the Ship Hotel and in the forbidding church of 1726, to which age belongs Joshua Christall's charming watercolour of a Dolgelley milkmaid. But if we would learn something of Dolgelley in the eighteenth century we must turn to the nine handwritten volumes of Elizabeth Baker's *Diary* in the National Library at Aberystwyth. Elizabeth Baker left London for Dolgelley in 1770 to attend to her mining interests, but that venture proving abortive, she obtained a post as secretary to Hugh Vaughan, squire of the nearby Hengwrt. It is to her eight-year diary, as to a few documents such as the *Henblas Household Accounts* and the letters of the Morris brothers, that we are indebted for some lively and informative cameos of eighteenth-century Wales.

It may well be that the true glory of Wales is not Snowdonia but an area of some fifteen miles radius about Dolgelley. Peacock, in *Crotchet Castle*, refers to this area as "the land of all that is beautiful in nature, and all that is lovely in women", and the engirdling mountains caused old

Fuller to remark that "the walls of Dolgelley are three miles high". Eastward runs the road to Dinas Mawddwy, north-eastward the road to Bala and northward that to Ffestiniog, all ways of escape into the mountains.   The last road skirts the Afon Wen, which is worth penetrating for the waterfalls, leaving the chameleon slopes of Penrhos eastward, and beyond the picturesque Tyn-y-Groes hotel it follows the Eden valley to the artificial lake of Trawsfynydd, sunk in desolate moorlands.   The immediate environs of Dolgelley are rich in those scenic features eulogised in the guide-books, in those Precipice and Torrent Walks which in spite of the boosting are intrinsically worth while.   And in this area is Cymmer Abbey, another Cistercian foundation of the thirteenth century, with some fragments of a church which did not conform to the traditional plan, due, perhaps, to the exigencies of continuous warfare in the district. The blue Mawddach estuary is the jewel of the area and it is inescapable, almost always in view from this land of high belvederes (89).   From the northern bank mountains and sea are drawn together and a phalanx of mountains lies ahead, Moel Cynwch overshadowed by the high crags of Cader.   There are summer hydrangeas in the hamlets here, and in the hills are abandoned gold-mines.   We must contrive to avoid Barmouth, a granite centipede sprawling along the shores of this Welsh Dragenfels, though we would see its mother-church at Llanaber for the sake of its setting between hill and sea, the characteristic thirteenth-century work, the single eastern lancet and the unusual prodigality of clustered shafts.

Northward lies Harlech and, beyond again, the magic of Snowdonia (90).   Across the Ysgethin is Llanddwywe, with a late-Perpendicular church containing a chapel of 1615 and a monument to its founder, Gruffydd Vaughan.   These particular Vaughans, one of whom, a Member of Parliament for Merioneth *temp*. Charles I, was so fat that the folding-doors of the House of Commons had always to be opened for him, lived at Cors-y-Gedol at the end of a long avenue of lime-trees. The house, now a hostel, is of *c*. 1536, though somewhat altered, and is in the style of most manor-houses of the period, Plas Rhiwaedog, Plas Mawr, etc.   The gatehouse was added in 1630 and, with the chapel, is rashly attributed to the apparently prolific Inigo Jones.   The reef-like St. Patrick's Causeway projects seaward and the soft hills of the Lleyn peninsula now rise above Cardigan Bay.   Eastward are the heathery slopes of the twin Rhinogs, wild plants growing between their chaotic, immense boulders, in the purlieus of which are several tarns worth seeking out.   From Llanbedr an excellent excursion may be made along the wooded valley of the Artro to the heather-girdled lake of Cwm Bychan; at the head of the valley are the so-called Roman Steps, a primitive staircase of rude slabs of rock and of problematical origin, perhaps a medieval packway.   Beyond the wild defile of Bwlch Drws Ardudwy, one of the celebrated entrances into the mountains of Ardudwy, is Maes-y-Garnedd,

72  The Mawddach Estuary near Barmouth, Merionethshire

73  Harlech Castle, Merionethshire

a timber-framed cottage in which was born Colonel John Jones, brother-in-law of Cromwell, who was executed as a regicide in 1660.

The small town of Harlech is wholly dominated by its dark feudal castle, crowning a bold crag at the head of the estuary of the Traeth Bach and overlooking the broad angle of Tremadoc Bay (91). This is one of the last and grandest of the Edwardian fortresses, and, like Beaumaris, it shows the development of principles of defence suitable to the site. It is certain that the Frankish or Syriac genius, Master James de St. George, *magister operacionum regis in Wallia*, did much work here, as he did at Rhuddlan, Flint, Conway and Beaumaris, and it may be held that since he was the architect of Rhuddlan he must also have designed Harlech. It is a rectangular fortress enclosed by two lines of walls forming inner and middle baileys, while the outer bailey is conveniently formed by a rocky, precipitous slope. The eastern or more vulnerable side is well fortified by an ingenious gatehouse and flanking bastions. Though it was taken by Glyndowr it was an almost impregnable fortress, and its later history was not of Welsh against English but of Lancastrian versus Yorkist, the Lancastrian castellan, Sir Dafyd ap Jevin ap Einion, being finally starved out after a long siege. These doughty warriors were men of words as well as of action and there was about them a fine air of braggadocio. When called upon by Herbert, Earl of Pembroke, to surrender, Sir Dafyd retorted that he had held a castle in France until all the old women in Wales had heard of it, and now he intended to hold Harlech until all the old women in France heard of it. This recalls the brilliant repartee provoked at Château Gaillard, where Philip Augustus haughtily remarked to Richard Coeur de Lion, "I will take Château Gaillard if it be made of iron," to which Richard retorted, "I will hold it, were it made of butter." But Harlech, seen by moonlight or in storm, is the very stuff of romance, even if we no longer see it as James Ward painted it early last century. And if it is a symbol of English might, it is also a badge of Welsh courage; here is the holy ground of Welsh arms, and there is no Welshman that passes but his pulse must quicken.

The walls and mountain-fences all about are of stone, and beyond the alluvial flat of Morfa Harlech is Talsarnau, lying near the beautiful estuary of the Dwyryd and Glaslyn rivers, the Traeth Bach or 'little shore'. The tongue of land jutting into these waters is Penrhyn Point, a domain of azalea, mimosa and rhododendrons in which the Ivory Towers of Portmeirion have been cunningly contrived. But we enter the Vale of Ffestiniog and arrive at Maentwrog, a village in a lovely setting. Many of the early-nineteenth-century houses have rustic wood galleries in Tyrolean fashion, and Plas Tan-y-Bwlch, across the valley, is nicely framed in the space between two cottage ranges. The church here though largely modern is wilfully pretty, with yew-trees about its shingled tower. Thomas Love Peacock, whose *Headlong Hall* and *The Misfortunes of Elphin* are novels of Snowdonia, married the vicar's daughter, Jane Gruffydd, who, to quote Mrs. Gisborne, the friend of Shelley, "seems to be a very good-natured, simple, unaffected, untaught, prettyish Welsh girl". A daughter of this union became the wife of George Meredith. Northward, looking up the village street, is the peak of Moel Bach, and following the well-wooded valley one comes at length to Ffestiniog.

This grey village sits on the verge of a green moorland plateau bordering the Vale of Ffestiniog, and the valley of the Cynfael which cuts across the south. It is the centre of a little-known and glorious mountain-locked country which has its moods of sheer joy and infinite depression. It is a land of waterfalls, and standing in the village square in the quiet of evening one hears their massed, concerted roar. Within a two-mile radius are a dozen or so of these falls; the Rhaiadr Cwm with its six cascades; the Rhaiadr Ddu and the Raven Falls, all in the Cynfael valley; the two falls of the Afon Gamalt, slightly north-east in the Manods; two in Coed Pengwern; two more on the nearby Afon Goedol; and several others above Tan-y-Bwlch. The area is also surprisingly rich in historic houses. There are Tyddyn, once the home of Archdeacon Prys, whose Welsh translation of the Psalter is still in use, and Cynfael Fawr, the home of Hugh Lluyhd, bard and mystic, both of the early seventeenth century. Across the sixteenth-century Pont Dol-y-moch is the coeval house of that name, with dormers and tall stacks and open timber roof, and farther down the valley is the lonely farmhouse of Ddualt, perched high above the river. The latter is a problematical building and its earliest portions include some curious features, the arches of its tiny court or vestibule having heads of rough-hewn unmortared slabs recalling the construction of the 'Flemish' houses about St. David's. It is worth climbing to Ddualt for the view embracing the valley southward. (A novel exploration of the area between Blaenau Ffestiniog and Portmadoc may be made by following the disused track of the Ffestiniog Light Railway, laid in 1836 to carry slate to the harbour, a lofty passage of some thirteen miles which contrives to make some tricky negotiations of some wild and awkward spots.) Perhaps the most characteristic feature of the area is the *tyddyn* or Welsh farmhouse, for though there is little arable land, sheep-farming is fairly prosperous. These farmhouses are often of some age and are invariably constructed of rough-hewn slate blocks from the Ordovician rock. Such is Bwlch Iocyn (until recently the home of Arthur Koestler), with its dairy, which must be one of the last (probably *the* last) places in Wales in which butter was churned by a wheel driven by a dog-team. Some of the smaller farms and cottages have interiors which recall descriptions in the *Mabinogion*—not the elaborate interiors of the *Dream of Maxen Wledig* but a development of the simple, crude interiors of the *Dream of Rhonabwy*—for the fire is made against the gable-end and the beds are placed on opposite sides of the house. There are warm brown oak dressers and chests, settles and

74   Cader Idris, Merionethshire
*From the painting by Richard Wilson (1774)*

75   Snowdon, Caernarvonshire, with the Mountain Railway in the foreground

76  Bala, Merionethshire, from across the Valley of the Dee

77  Rhobell Fawr and Llanfachreth, near Dolgelley, Merionethshire

grandfather-clocks, three-legged tables and chairs, a garnish of pewter and an array of china guarded by fiery china dogs. In some places the living-room is yet partitioned off from the kitchen by a panelled screen, as at Hafod Yspytty, a remote farmhouse in the wild Manods. This is an excellent example of cruck-construction in a slate house of *c.* 1500. The site is of some antiquity, for tradition refers to a fourteenth-century hospice on the pilgrims' road to Bardsey, and the lawn rises over a pre-historic burial chamber. The latter doorway of the house has an arched wooden lintel inscribed in Greek *Peace to this House*, and the original screen dividing the lower rooms is richly moulded and contains an arched doorway at each end, while stone staircases and massive ingle-nooks are all original. An interesting feature is the open timber roof with pierced quatrefoils framed above the truss, an unusual design which I have nowhere else encountered, though I have seen similar ones at Wigmore Grange in Herefordshire and Tretower Court in Brecknock. Today Hafod is a charming hermitage cared for by Mark Sontag, Austrian-born painter, who has added a studio and has designed and painted the Austrian furniture gracing this unique home. Sontag holds five hundred acres of 'rock and bog', a country so primitive that on my arrival a large dog-fox, shot that morning, lay near the threshold.

The approaches to these lonely houses are rough, stony tracks, and as I turned back in a hired car Jones the Garage nodded towards the flesh-pots of Blaenau Ffestiniog and murmured "Civilisation". Blaenau, however, is best ignored, for it is the Martha to the Mary of its sister Ffestiniog and is dominated by slate quarrying, by the ugly black gashes in the mountainsides, by the indifferent terraced houses and by the slate-piles oddly tenanted by roaming sheep. The Oakley slate mine is the largest in the world, but today these workings are half-empty, for the younger men hold back from fear of silicosis. From Ffestiniog the road to Bala crosses the Migneint moorlands and skirts the foothills of the great Arenig Fawr, a barren mass that looks like a bit of Ireland. We would do better to return along the Vale of Ffestiniog as far as Maen-twrog and then cross the short, straight causeway into Tan-y-Bwlch. The *plas*, perched high against an arras of hanging woodlands, has an Elizabethan nucleus with embattled walls and turrets which are largely Victorian, and one envies the occupants for the grand view from the terrace. In the hamlet below it there are some homely groups, a farm-house with bell-cote, an old mill and water-wheel and a pheasantry. The road behind the estate runs beside the rhododendron-fringed Llyn Mair and into the isolated hamlet of Rhydd, the Moelwyns now rising beyond. On the way to Llanfrothen the mountains range all about, except where, away and below, curls the silver ribbon of the head of Traeth Bach, but we drop down at last into the hamlet of Garreg. Here is a pagoda-like tower which is quite unexpected, but after seeing a few more such hybrids in the district it is gradually forced in upon us that all this is the work of Clough Williams-Ellis, who, like a medieval bishop of St. David's, has brought a hint of sunny Italy to this terrain. There is more of this imaginative architecture in Plas Brondanw, partly seventeenth century, with terraced gardens and clipped yews and views of Snowdon and Cynicht. But the spectral pyramidal peak of Cynicht is best seen from Garreg Bridge.

We have descended to the level, green Traeth Mawr, surrounded on three sides by lofty hill ridges, which stretches from the estuary to a point below Beddgelert and from the foothills of the Moelwyns to the valley of the Glaslyn. The hump and saddle of the Moelwyns now appear eastward—and always that bright cone of Cynicht—and Cwm Croesor will take you into the heart of them. The indifferent pasturage stretches almost to Pont Aberglaslyn, which springs over the velvet-bouldered river, fringed with conifers and backed by towering grey cliffs. The pass is among the glories of Wales, and in a little while it opens out to reveal the mountain village of Beddeglert. For we are in Caernarvon, the very name an incantation.

# X

## BEDDGELERT THE LLEYN PENINSULA CAERNARVON AND THE NORTH COAST THE SNOWDON FOREST THE CONWY LLUGWY AND LLEDR VALLEYS

BEDDGELERT, squatting grey-walled between the mountains and laved by three impetuous streams, Glaslyn, Colwen and Gwynant, bestows its benison upon those who seek beauty in minor tones and *adagio* moods. There are splashes of colour in roses climbing cottage-walls, in columbines, bluebells and foxgloves fringing the floor of the valley, and in the wand-like white birch and ash which diaper the foot-hills. The prim houses have Gothic casements of last century, and the stuccoed Goat Hotel is of *c.* 1800, but few are of any age. The house now called Llewelyn's Cottage is probably of the seventeenth century and was formerly the Ty Isaf inn, presumably the hostelry in which Bingley was bitten by a legion of marauding fleas; here was kept a quart tankard, and he who quaffed his beer at a draught could charge it to the squire. The inn signboard remains, luridly portraying the Gelert legend for which the village became celebrated. Much doubt has been cast upon the authenticity of this canine sob-story, a story paralleled almost exactly in Sanscrit literature, while Baring-Gould went to great pains to cite other examples. No matter; for any pretext which brings us to Beddgelert is welcome. A. J. Froude was discerning enough to live in the Nant Gwynant, where he wrote some of his best essays and entertained Matthew Arnold and Charles Kingsley. On the far edge of the lake, above which are grouped the peaks of Lliwedd, Y Wyddfa and Crib Goch, is Hafod Lwyfog, the manor-house of *c.* 1638 and the home of John Williams, goldsmith to James I. Several of the harpists of this house acted as mountain-guides, and guiding became a tradition in Beddgelert, attract-ing at least one savant, William Lloyd, the schoolmaster, who would act in this capacity. Lloyd seems to have been quite a character; he collected crystals and fossils and was also a dealer in hosiery. He died in 1804, or, as a contemporary writer would have it, "he finally emerged from all sublunary avocations to the regions beyond the grave".

As yet Beddgelert has changed but little, though whey is no longer drunk here and the coffin-plates of deceased parishioners are no longer hung above their pews in the church. Most of all, perhaps, one misses the horn that sounded among these hills, summoning the shepherds to their meals in the lofty *hafodtai* (as it yet does or did until a few years ago on Exmoor). Standing upon the footbridge and looking up the valley towards Nant Gwynant, across the swift, turbulent Glaslyn, one feels and hopes that it never will change. And our last glimpse of Beddgelert shall be of its bell-coted church, largely thirteenth-century work, with its elegant eastern triplet, reproduced in miniature in the west end of Llanfrothen church and to be encountered again in Conway. From the thirteenth century Augustinian canons here read their breviaries, but long before that time the Celtic culdees held this valley.

To reach the Lleyn peninsula one must take the north side of the Traeth Mawr from Pont Aberglaslyn. The reclamation of this land by William Maddocks early last century has robbed us of what must have been an enchanting scene, for the blue waters of the estuary came right up to the mountainsides. By some strange process of casuistry Shelley persuaded himself that the scheme was commendable, and he opened the subscription list for the completion of the Portmadoc dyke with one hundred pounds. Nor is it any consolation to know that Maddocks (who has his monument in Llanfrothen church) was finally compelled to flee to France to avoid his creditors. Shelley and Harriet lived for a while in a cottage in the grounds of Tan-yr-Allt, Maddocks' urbane Regency villa; here the poet wrote much of *Queen Mab*, and he wrote in a letter to the unmentionable Hogg: "We simple people live here in a cottage extensive and tasty enough for the villa of an Italian prince."

Tremadoc is a planned town or village of *c.* 1805, its square penned in by a formidable mass of rock. The Town Hall, decorated with the whimsical paterae and figure-heads of the period, is the focal point of this square of modest cottages. Nearby is the theatre of 1808, with Roman Doric portico, now a chapel, and almost opposite is a curious and ugly Gothic church. In one of the later houses, by a mere fluke of circumstance, was born T. E. Lawrence, the son of an Anglo-Irish squire and a Highland Scottish mother. Avoiding Portmadoc, largely created by the enterprising Maddocks, one comes to Criccieth and the bold gatehouse and flanking drums of its ruined castle perched upon a green hill overhanging the sea.

We are on the edge of the Lleyn and we would do well to make a detour to Llangybi, which indeed has nothing but the ancient well of a saintly hermit, so old and eloquent of the humble beginnings of this country that it is an excellent introduction to the peninsula. For if we would understand the Lleyn—and Wales—aright, we must go back to the fifth and sixth centuries, back to Celtic Christianity, as yet undiluted by the Latin strain, back to the *clas* and the hermitage, to dawn immersions in icy water and fasting on fried seaweed and the whole process of self-

78 The Screen at Leeswood Hall, Flintshire (*c.* 1730)

79 The Bridge Gates at Emral, Flintshire (*c.* 1725)

80 The Forecourt Gates, Chirk Castle,
Denbighshire (1719) (*left*)

IRON WORK BY THE DAVIES
BROTHERS OF BERSHAM
(*fl.* 1702–55)

81   Looking towards Bardsey Island, Caernarvonshire

82   Morfa Nevin, Caernarvonshire

immolation, back to holy wells and chapels and relics and cults. Here upon the steps of St. Gybi's well we stand on the brink of a lost age, an age which, for all its fantastic and savage discipline, yet moulded the refinements of *Homo sapiens* as we now know him. The Lleyn may well be one of the last refuges of Welsh traditions, for the railway ends at Pwllheli, and in this promontory many people have *dim Saesneg*, 'no English', the family often climbs to bed in the *croglloft*, and many pre-Reformation customs, the viaticum ceremony among them, survive as ritual gestures. But we must reach out beyond slovenly Pwllheli to the claw-tip of Penkilan Head. Within this area lies a group of primitive villages with saffron-washed cottages and venerable churches—Llanbedrog, lying snugly on the shore beneath a wooded promontory, Abersoch, with its creeks and sand-dunes facing the deserted, guillemot-held islands of St. Tudwal (is this the Welsh Tudwal who became bishop of the Breton Tréguier?), Llangian, with its lonely churchyard, and Llanengan, with its rood-screen spread-eagled across the entire church and a lych-gate where is kept the parish bier. The entrance into Aberdaron on a stormy night can be startling, the road dropping abruptly into the village to reveal a seascape lying below, on the edge of which appear the cradle-roofs of the church and a churchyard crowded with flat, regimented tombs, table-like, all glistening with rain and quite spectral.

The fishing-village of Aberdaron in a cove of Aberdaron Bay was until recently one of the most primitive of Welsh villages. It has raised generations of hardy seamen, and men here can construct a fourteen-feet dinghy inside three weeks. Dick Aberdaron, a 'nine-days' wonder' who wrote a manuscript dictionary of Welsh, Greek and Hebrew, was the son of such a local carpenter. The village is white-harled and is bridged across its streams, and its church is mainly fifteenth-century work with some earlier features, bare and aisleless but having a good east window with ogival lights. Half of the churchyard was washed away in a great storm early last century, and a new church was built inland; then someone had the bright idea of building a retaining wall about the churchyard, and the Romanesque hybrid, its Welsh Bible still upon the lectern, has been deserted ever since. The islanders of Bardsey contrive to land here once a week, but there are often many weeks before these courageous people can negotiate Bardsey Sound, a nasty piece of water with the venomous lash of a serpent. The voyage from Aberdaron is high adventure, a journey into wonderland, and the mountain that rises out of the sea is like a mirage. This island of Ynys Enlli is best seen from Braich-y-Pwll, its heathery bluff falling into the sea, and the crystal waters of its ancient well of St. Mary draped with a luminous ribbon of seaweed. Beyond lies Bardsey (81), rich in the odour of sanctity, as the monkish chroniclers have it. Only a thirteenth-century tower remains of an abbey which seems never to have been assimilated with Benedictines or Augustinians and which to all appearances maintained its autonomy as a Celtic settlement of culdees up to the Dissolution. Today Bardsey is tenanted by a patriarchal community which survives by hard farming eked out by a traffic in the steel-blue crabs and baby-pink lobsters. A single road runs from the stony uplands to the rich lowland soil, and the granite farmhouses are paired off. There is the scent of clover, rusty lichens mantle the cliffs, sea-fowl wheel about the mountain, and out to sea there is the head of a bouncing seal.

The north of the peninsula has landscapes akin to those of rural Ireland, an impression enhanced by the habits and characteristics of the people. In the hay-fields one notes such pleasant mannerisms as the stacking of ricks with corbie-stepped 'gables'. Black cattle roam the undulating pastures. The whale-back of Cefn Amlwch is covered with crimson bell-heather in early autumn, and below it lies Bryncroes, where the church contains curious seventeenth-century wooden memorials to local squires; while westward is the church of Llangwadl, with three equal naves separately roofed and gabled. At nearby Bodvel Hall was born Mrs. Thrale, who fell out with Dr. Johnson over her marriage to Piozzi, but whose *Anecdotes of the late Samuel Johnson* provides an admirable portrait of that sage. The volcanic-looking mass of Garn Fadryn dominates the heart of the Lleyn, and in the sheltered oak and beech-studded valleys round about are charmingly placed Llandudwen and Llaniestyn. Above lie Ceidio and Edyrn, both with interesting old churches retaining their medieval roof-trusses. The deserted haven of Porth Dinlleyn on its sickle-shaped bay almost became what Holyhead now is, the principal mail-port for Ireland, and neighbouring Nevin, where Edward I held a famous tournament to celebrate the strength of his mailed fist in Wales, was until recently a shipbuilding town, but the only brig one is liable to see here now crowns the church spire. Beyond the triune-peaked Rivals is Llanaelhaiarn, where we return to the mysteries of the Celtic Church, for the great *ffynnon Aelhaiarn* is the sire of all Welsh wells (excepting the shrine of Holywell in Flint), with a causeway and seat around it. Most of the early churches of Caernarvonshire had their accompanying holy wells, and in many parishes the *gwylmabsant*, or patronal feast-day, was observed well into the Victorian era. The church is of the eastern-transeptal type, with a primitive gabled façade having an unusually tall bell-cote, a rood-screen with original traceried heads, and an eastern window of three equal lancets, probably derived from the Beddgelert triplet. In the last century the knitting and story-telling evenings in the village were known as *pilnos*, or 'rush-peeling nights', for peeling rushes for lights was a necessary labour, and rush-holders are frequently encountered, as antiques, in farmhouses.

We have left the Lleyn, and among the holly trees between the heights of Gryn Goch and the sea is Clynnog Fawr. Though there are white-washed cottages and attractive Georgian inn and parsonage, the church is of such proportions and elegance that it dominates this lovely place

83   Clynnog Fawr Church, Caernarvonshire

84   Aberconway (*c.* 1400), the oldest house in Conway

84. Caernarvon, showing the Castle, town walls, mediaeval streets and houses of the later period. Wales

(83). The original, founded by St. Beuno, c. 616, was the chapel of yet another *clas*, but by the thirteenth century it had become collegiate, and the existing structure is an excellent example of early-sixteenth-century work. The tower and the fenestration are remarkably fine, and the building contains a vaulted sacristy, stalls and book-desks with linen-fold panelling, a plain rood-screen, an Elizabethan screen below the tower, and crocketed ogival sedilia. The most interesting feature, however, is the chapel of St. Beuno, set obliquely to the church and connected by a barrel-vaulted passage, on the site of the original *myfyr* of the saint and formerly containing his shrine. From Pen-y-groes the Vale of Nantlle, with its chain of reddish cliffs, may be followed to Rhyd-ddu, from where the fine mountain-lake of Quellyn may be reached. But we are bound for Caernarvon, beyond Llanllyfni church, with its eastern transepts, and beyond the wooded Glynllifon Park. The low green land of Anglesey has been in view for some while, and at Llanwnda, beyond the alluvial flats, there are glimpses of the Menai Strait.

The first downward glance at Caernarvon Castle towering above the Seiont is a revelation (85), but only when one has walked, dwarf-like, in the lee of its beetling walls does one realise the power of this chilly monster, a more oppressive tyrant than anything we have yet seen. For feudal grandeur there is nothing in western Europe to excel it. From Harlech to the Krak des Chevaliers in Tripoli, from Caernarvon to Constantinople, with its three-mile triple wall and a hundred flanking towers, seems a far cry; yet it was from precisely such places that the Crusaders returned with the idea of the concentric fortress. Its further development must be traced in the tactical measures of Richard I at Château Gaillard and in the lessons learned at first hand by Edward himself amid the *bastides* of Gascony. To Walter of Hereford, master-mason, must be attributed the design of Caernarvon, though it was building from 1285 to 1322. It is shaped like an hour-glass, comprising two courts with a total of thirteen towers, of which the Eagle Tower is one of the largest of all medieval towers. There were two major and three subordinate entrances, and the defensive principles of medieval gateways reached their zenith in the King's Gate. The original walls of the borough, built immediately *before* the castle, remain almost in entirety, and the church of St. Mary, built on the curtain walls in the north-west angle, was probably the garrison-chapel. From the promenade and the sea the illusion is perfect—here is a genuine walled city, as compact as Carcassonne or Jerusalem or Avila in Spain (85).

Once inside the town, however, and one breathes the air of the late eighteenth and early nineteenth centuries, for that was the age of rebuilding, and the two main gatehouses have undergone some metamorphosis; the East Gate indeed is now crowned by a Victorian guildhall in Baronial Gothic with bartizan turrets. Yet the plan of the town preserves the cross-streets set at regular distances of the original borough, and the area within the walls corresponds exactly with Speed's map of 1610. Though there is a little earlier fabric, the houses are largely Georgian, including some sober examples in Castle Street, Bank Quay and Church Street. Without the walls there is the porticoed Royal Hotel, while almost one side of Castle Square, though dated 1834, is a little earlier in idiom than the date suggests. And Castle Square is the hub of Caernarvon; here are serried ranks of 'buses bearing the names of their destinations, all names of magic—Llanberis, Beddgelert, Capel Curig; here is Goscombe John's statue of Lloyd George, with his leonine head; and from here the vast coffee-coloured castle walls and finger-turrets (rendered perfect by Anthony Salvin last century) stretch almost to the sea, along the harbour front, no longer bristling with the masts of ships loading Nantlle slates. There is drama here, though perhaps we shall never see such drama as Paul Sandby created in his picture of Caernarvon burning by night.

There is one aspect of Caernarvon's past social life that we cannot overlook—the meetings of the Calvinist 'jumpers', who here assembled by their thousands well into the last century.

"They persuade themselves that they are involuntarily acted upon by some divine impulse; and becoming intoxicated with this imagined inspiration, they utter their rapture and their triumph with such wildness and incoherence—with such gesticulation and vociferation as set all reason and decorum at defiance . . . at length one among the crowd, wrought up to a pitch of ecstasy, starts and commences the jumping, using at intervals some expression of praise or triumph. . . . Men and women indiscriminately, cry and laugh, jump and sing, with the wildest extravagance.

That their dress becomes deranged or the hair dishevelled is no longer an object of attention. And their raptures continue till, spent with fatigue of mind and body, the women are frequently carried out in a state of apparent insensibility."

I quote the above account, cited by Bingley late in the eighteenth century, because it corresponds in every detail with the behaviour in a negro mission which I visited in New York's Harlem.

On the road to Bettws Garmon and Beddgelert is the church of Llanbeblig, with a Tudor crow-stepped tower and a peculiar ground-plan. Nearby is the excavated site of the Roman Segontium of normal Flavian type and rebuilt in stone early in the second century. The road to Llanberis is the way into the heart of the Snowdon Forest, though much of it is an ordeal, for the new Llanberis is as ugly as sin, the glistening coal-black slate piles falling sheer into Lake Padarn. Here is a Victorian church designed by Arthur Baker, a pupil of the elder Scott, and a school which specialises in the craft of quarrying and dressing slates to sizes known as 'queens', 'duchesses', 'countesses' and 'ladies'. Dolbadarn

86, 87 Details of Monuments at Gresford (1797) (*left*)
and Llanrhaiadr. Denbighshire (early eighteenth-century)

88 Llanrhaiadr Church, Denbighshire : an early eighteenth-century Monument

80  Llanberis, Caernarvonshire, looking towards the Pass

Castle, a solitary thirteenth-century juliet in which Owen Goch, brother
of Llewelyn the Great, spent twenty imprisoned years of utter darkness,
crowns a knoll on the shores of Llyn Peris. This lower lake is sombre
and strangely appealing in spite of the quarries tiered upon the slopes of
Elidyr Fawr. And below is old Llanberis, with its crude medieval
church squatting near the head of the pass. In this wind-swept village
one recalls Margaret Uch Evan, a celebrated character of the eighteenth
century to whom Pennant paid homage, for this extraordinary Amazon
wrestled, rowed, shot, fished, hunted and fiddled, and she was blacksmith, cobbler, joiner, boat-builder and harp-maker.

The pass of Llanberis, a sullen defile strewn with moraines (89), lies
beneath Snowdon itself. Here at last is the heart of Eryri, morose
enough except when vagaries of weather change its texture and bathe its
pinnacles in glory, yet mythopœic and immutable. The naked walls of
Glyder Fawr rise northward out of the pass, and, opposite, crag upon
crag, ledge upon ledge, tower away to the ultimate peaks; to glacial
Cwm Glas and the precipice of Crib-y-Ddysgl, where nestle coy mid-
summer cushions of moss-campion, the blushing mountain sorrel, the
white starry saxifrage and prolific clumps of thrift; to the cracked pinnacles of Crib Goch, Wyddfa and Lliwedd, where is Snowdon's most
awful precipice; to the black still waters of Llyn Llydaw and Glaslyn and
Du'r Arddu, overhung by a rock bastion moulded like a blancmange.
In the gleaming-white hamlet of Gorphwysfa is a delectable inn, a
refuge from the tempestuous heights, but not until we reach Pen-y-
Gwryd do we recover from that near-claustrophobia inspired by the
pass. A night at Pen-y-Gwryd is a *sine qua non* of a tour of Snowdonia.
You will probably trip over ropes and boots, you will hang your own
soaking clothes in the drying-room, and you will be politely requested
at a certain point beyond the door to remove your nailed boots. The
conversation will be of saddles, arêtes, cirques, pitons, *mousquetons*,
running belays, the 'Cambridge anchor' and the Yukon pack-frame, for
the jargon of the mountaineer is second in technical complexity only to
the language of the balletomane. The halcyon days of the inn were
those when Victorian Harry Owen was host, when Charles Kingsley
introduced it into his *Two Years Ago*, and when, at the end of Hilary, there
was an annual exodus of undergraduates from Oxford. Yet Pen-y-Gwryd
remains an appropriate place for meditation upon the long history of
this area, and looking through the windows across to Moel Siabod, the
mountainous skies slowly filling with stars, one recalls the long cavalcade
of distinguished itinerarists. There is Samuel Johnson, an unkind Goth;
Richard Fenton, the historian of Pembrokeshire; good old Thomas
Pennant, the naturalist; Bingley, the expert botanist; Samuel Warner,
the parson from Bath; Roscoe, the Romantic from Liverpool; and
George Borrow, the boisterous Bible-thumper. Theodore Watts-
Dunton, whom some writers have made out to be Swinburne's Cerebus,

wrote descriptive passages of much beauty in *Aylwin*, a novel of Snowdon which, in spite of the romantic hocus-pocus about 'dukkeripen', puts the atmosphere across in an uncannily true manner.

From Pen-y-Gwryd we follow the desolate valley between Glyder Fach, down which pour numerous little *afons* like the dripping saliva from snorting beasts, and Moel Siabod. Siabod is best seen from Capel Curig, where its slopes are dappled with scrub, purple moor grass and bog myrtle. Capel Curig is happily strung out at the confluence of three valleys and is hemmed in by mountains on all sides. Its Victorian church is another of those Romanesque buildings by Paley and Austin, interesting *pasticheurs*, and its old church, reticent and solitary, is one of the smallest in the area and retains its original double-square plan. Modern hostelries provide some measure of the village's later development, but the solid yellow-ochre washed Royal Hotel was the first of the dynasty and is celebrated for its Welsh mutton. And for the benefit of the gourmet let it be recorded that Wales can still offer such specialities as the *slapan* of Caernarvon, the *crempog* or pancake of Merioneth, the *picws màli* or bruised oatmeal cake with butter-milk of Anglesey, the *sucan* or thin flummery of North Wales (known as *bwdran* in the south), genuine old-fashioned, well-hung, sweet-cured hams, fruit pies, bakestone cakes and laver-bread.

Between the rock-strewn foothills of the Glyders and those of the Carnedds, the Holyhead road follows the sparkling Llugwy, shaded by alders and pranked with bright green mosses and the white-flowered crowfoot. Beyond Lake Ogwen, above which rises the dark peak of Tryfan, is the rough approach to Cwm Idwal and the awesome tarn of Llyn Idwal damned by glacial moraines and overhung by the main precipice of Glyder Fawr. Nearby is the vertical fissure of Twll Ddu, veritably a 'Devil's Kitchen', rich in the rare plants and flowers which are to be found in so many of these gullies—saxifrage, meadow rue, the globe flower and the rarer mountain avens. Across the Ogwen, the marshy green Nant Ffrancon brings us to the purlieus of more slate-quarrying country and into Bethesda, which, like Blaenau Ffestiniog, has sold its beauty for the proverbial mess of pottage.

Near the village of Llanllechid is Cochwillan Hall, a house of *c.* 1500 containing a fine hammer-beam roof. Here lived the Williams, a family which produced John Williams—"hasty, hot Welsh Williams", Carlyle called him—the militant Archbishop of York, whose portrait yet hangs in St. John's College at Cambridge. Williams bought Penrhyn Castle, formerly the home of the Griffiths, who gave a daughter in marriage to Henry VII's Breton son, De Velville, though the monster that now cocks a feudal eye upon its model village of Llandegai is a hybrid of 1836. Of grey Mona marble, it is pure pastiche, neo-Norman, with a five-storeyed tower based upon the keep of Rochester, painted glass windows by Willement, a dark crypt-like chapel and an impressive hall

with curiously shaped arches.    Thomas Hopper was the architect, though
Samuel Wyatt seems to have had a hand in the building, as he did, or
one of the Wyatts did—for the entire family seems to have worked for
Lord Penrhyn—in that of the model cottages clustered about the church.
The latter, at the end of an avenue of limes, is cruciform with central
tower, and contains a mural tablet to Archbishop Williams and a monument in conventional Attic manner by Westmacott.

Though the approaches to Bangor are pleasant, the town is disappointing, except where it impinges on the Menai Strait and one looks from a
terraced height across to the towered mansions on the Anglesey shore.
The town is dominated by the Jacobean-cum-Renaissance buildings of
the University College, one of the four constituent colleges of the University of Wales, which is today crowded with the sons and daughters of
Welsh working-class families.    One can find little to say in praise of
Bangor Cathedral: as a parish church it is interesting, as a cathedral it is
unlovely and unworthy, tenebrous and chill, the plaster peeling from
its faded walls.    This is the third church on the site, though it was ruined
during the Edwardian campaigns and subsequently rebuilt at various
periods.    The building is quite parochial in character, but retains a few
notable features, the tracery of the tower and clerestory windows, for
example, and the well-executed buttresses of the south transept, which
suggest the craftsmanship of Chester masons—but the whole church
must be largely regarded as the work of Sir Gilbert Scott.    Nearby is a
picturesque building which was formerly the Episcopal Palace, embodying
a little early fabric but mainly Georgian work, yellow-ochre washed with
'Gothick' casements and containing a moulded plaster ceiling of that
period.    In Vaynol Park, a little southward, is a good late-sixteenth-
century manor-house nicely grouped with formal garden, great barn
and chapel of 1596, the last having affinities with the manorial chapel of
Gwydir Uchaf.

The coastal road from Bangor to Conway is flanked by green meadows
rolling down to the Strait and by occasional small plantations of trees,
against which white, feathery clouds of gulls make a pleasant contrast.
The lofty Carnedds now fall well back, and at Aber a narrow glen hung
with cascades cuts across their northern foothills.    Near here is Pen-y-
Bryn, the remnant of an old house which is traditionally the home of
both Lewellyn the Great and Llewelyn ap Gruffydd, with a barn which
shows some early local work.    The long, low smudge of Anglesey now
lies on the oiling waters of Conway Bay, and from the hinterland one sees
the sea hanging between thin forests and the distant island.    The Pen-
maenmawr headland is massive and arrogant enough to command a
transient respect, and beyond it is the old road into Conway through the
Sychnant Pass, a verdant defile trenched through rising moorlands, but
the direct road runs around the head of the Conwy estuary, the grey-
striped whale-back of the Great Orme rising on the far side.

Let your first impression of Conway be from the quays of this medieval burg, forgetting for a while the awful threat to demolish them in order that a new arterial road may more readily bring sophistry and false prophets to Eryri. The anchorage is crowded with craft, and a few trawlers nose their way out to sea. The fishermen tramp down under the old Water Gate and on to the quay, for there is work to be done and the mussels are piled high on the shingle. There is a hint of ballet or pantomime in the cream-glazed deep-sea boots of the mussel-gatherers. Nor is this the only element of surprise, for the entire place savours of the theatrical. Where else is there a bridge like this of Telford's springing directly on to a medieval castle laved by tidal water? And where in Britain is such a bracelet of walls and towers slipped about the homes of the people? (90) For these walls are all but perfect in their circuit, with twenty-one half-drum towers and three original gates climbing and bestraddling the streets, and in their lee has been set up a miniature Lourdes with grotto and sculptured *Via Crucis*. The castle, no longer clothed in the red valerian of recent years, is coeval in date and is the third of the Edwardian fortresses in Wales, though the first to be erected after the Conquest. Its massive walls are enfiladed by eight cylindrical towers, and though it is not an orthodox concentric castle, most of the principles of the concentric type are implied in its construction. It was part of Edwardian strategy to establish boroughs which were self-supporting and able to supply the needs of the garrison, and in the new planning the Cistercian abbey of Aberconway was moved to Maenan up-river. The conventual church which the monks abandoned is all that remains of Conway prior to the Edwardian conquest, though there is little of the original but the west front of the tower with its variant of the Latin triplet of Beddgelert and a richly carved mid-thirteenth-century doorway; other peculiarities include the lights of the tower and the quatrefoiled clerestory windows, while there is a good groined rood-loft.

Conway has some interesting old houses, among them the seventeenth-century Parlwr Mawr, a home of Archbishop Williams, Aberconway, a fifteenth-century merchant's house with the upper storey corbelled out on brackets (84), and an eighteenth-century cock-pit behind an antique-shop, which, judging from old prints, has lost a bow-windowed front. The cock-pit is an intriguing low, horse-shoe shaped building with tall 'Gothick' windows and a conical slate roof, and at Denbigh we shall have occasion to recall it. In Plas Mawr, now a museum, Conway has one of the finest manor-houses in Wales. Built for Robert Wynn between 1577 and 1580, it comprises gatehouse, courtyard and residence, the whole gabled and corbie-stepped in Flemish idiom. Internally it is rich in moulded plaster ceilings with zoological motifs—cranes, owls, swans, lions, griffins, stags and the bears and ragged staves of the Earl of Leicester. This plaster-work should be compared with that of the same period, perhaps by the same hand, at Maenan Hall and at Plastirion and Caer

90    The Town and Castle of Conway from the Walls

91   The Snowdon Range from Harlech, Merionethshire

Melwr near Llanrwst. Both Plas Mawr and the Castle Hotel have a wealth of the Welsh antique furniture depicted in Cornelius Varley's drawing of a farmhouse interior near Conway in 1802—the essentially Welsh *cwpwrdd deuddarn* and *cwpwrdd tridarn*, or two-piece and three-piece cupboards, the *cistie styffylog* or oatmeal chests, the *bord gron* or low, round three-legged stool, the settles and the oak boxed beds which recall the Dutch *pronk*, and the singular *clwyd fara* or cot-like crate which was suspended from the ceiling, one of which yet hangs in Plas Mawr.

Across the estuary (90) in the rock-studded Creuddyn peninsula is a group of houses of some interest. There is the Queen Anne-ish Marl, scene of Wilkie Collins's *The Haunted House*; Bodysgallen, with its pale Tudor gables; old Penrhyn; and Gloddaeth Hall, which turns its back upon Llandudno and looks down into a wooded hollow. This old home of the Mostyns is rich in original features of *c.* 1560, in its slate-paved hall with minstrels' gallery, stained-glass mullioned windows, great stone fireplace with Welsh inscription, and a dais painted with the arms of Queen Elizabeth, Leicester and the Mostyns. But we have already ventured too near to those unimaginative coastal resorts to which Christopher Hussey somewhere referred as being "dingily comatose". Rather would we return to Conway and leave it by way of Gyffin, with a church which is an excellent introduction to the area. The churches of Caernarvon are of singular interest, often combining early Welsh or British arrangements with English or Latin additions, the whole wielded together by the idiosyncrasies of post-Reformation reforms. Characteristic features— and they are largely confined to this region alone—range from the double-cube to eastern transepts, while most chancels have barrel-vaults of wood. Internal walls are invariably rough-faced or plastered, and the interiors are rather bare, filled only with furniture and other woodwork, much of which, benches, pews, pulpit, altar-table, etc., is of the seventeenth and eighteenth centuries. Thus there is some affinity between the inward appearances of these churches and those of the Netherlands, though here they are smaller and more intimate, filled with the odours of oil-lamps and candle-grease, the bouquet of wine-like wood, the scent of massed flowers, of wax and straw and mouldy hassocks and peeling plaster.

Gyffin's stream-side church has a painted wood barrel-vault over the sanctuary and a curious balustraded screen or altar-rail; the former is the only example of a painted vault in the area, though there is a good one at Llanelian below Colwyn Bay. Nearby is Llangelynin, with its solitary church in a grey, rough-walled enclosure adorned with white harebells beneath Craig Celynin, and here is a fine array of seventeenth- and eighteenth-century furniture and fittings. At Caerhun the church stands on the site of the Roman Conovium, near the Conwy river. Here is a double bell-cote which has the traditional straight ridge and gable in the middle, with a stiff, straight-armed crucifix below it, one of the oldest bell-cotes in Wales, for earlier there were only hand-bells, elaborate bells

of Celtic character such as that which Gildas gave to St. David.   Llanbedr
has whitewashed cottages and dark yews and an abundance of daffodils,
and its church has a single bell-cote with a crucifix similar to the above.
We are in the Conwy valley and soon reach Trefriw, another spa *manqué*,
to which steamers penetrate from Conway.   Here the rebuilt tiny parish
church is dwarfed by the nearby Methodist chapel, perched high on a
precipitate flight of steps which must be the Sabbath terror of the community.   From Trefriw it is worth while deviating along the pretty
Crafnant valley to Llyn Crafnant and, beyond it, the last lonely outpost
of Blaen-y-nant.   Nor should one omit the forest walk to Llanrhychwyn,
with its fort-like church crowning a rocky height, a church of primitive
construction, twin-naved, with an early square font and a delectable
Virgin and Child in brown and yellow cinquecento glass.

Llanrwst was one of the principal harp-making centres in Wales, and
harps were made here until 1810.   The instrument is engraved upon the
tomb-slabs of some of the craftsmen lying in the churchyard.   We shall
hear more of harps and harpists at Llangollen, but it is worth noting that
the lipe-work of the hooded harp-chairs of over a century ago provides
a transition to the wicker-work of coracles and cradles.   Llanrwst is
now an indifferent market-town, and its market-square no longer presents
the animated appearance of the charcoal-drawing by David Cox.   There
are the Victorian Town Hall, the Georgian Eagles Hotel, the seventeenth-
century almshouses and the parish church.   The last is of good Perpendicular work with a curious suggestion of Classical forms, and contains a rood-screen with a well groined loft.   The Gwydir Chapel, added
*c.* 1634, contains an elaborate lacunared roof, a pyramidal monument to
Sir Richard Wynn of Gwydir, Caroline desk and stalls carved with
human heads oddly resembling ancient Egyptians, and other curiosities.
From Llanrwst Bridge one looks up the Conwy towards Trefriw,
sheltering between the high wooded crags of Creigiau and Clunllom.
At sunset it is delightful, especially a mid-winter's sunset with a crimson-
and-emerald-ridged sky and banks of storm clouds, shot mauve and
magenta, riding above the hills.   This excellent bridge, of 1636, has been
referred to by some topographers as being feminine, though it has the
grace and strength of a male ballet-dancer and is perhaps hermaphroditic.
Adjoining it is a weathered old cottage of slate stone with door lintels and
window-frames of old oak.   Across the river is Gwydir Castle, which
when I last saw it was almost a shambles, reduced by fire for the third
time.   Its sixteenth-century porch-wing and tower remain, but the
Spanish leather-work and tapestries have long since been dispersed.   The
celebrated Dutch garden is a little jaded, the cedars and clipped yews less
spruce than formerly, and here one recalls the lost Dutch garden with
central summer-house at Maenan Abbey House.   The whole colourful
domain is best seen from the heights of Carreg y Gwalch, on a ledge of
which is Gwydir Uchaf, the dower house with its detached chapel of

1673. The latter is remarkable for its fusion of a late lingering Gothic with the Renaissance, and for its local craftsmanship, its coved ceiling with angels painted upon a blue background, its elaborate carved and painted gallery and its original fittings.    But the joy of Gwydir is its forest, especially lower down towards Bettws-y-Coed, where the Llugwy has a drop-curtain of sequoia, Norwegian spruce, Corsican and Scots pine, cypress and larch.

Where Conwy and Llugwy meet is Bettws-y-Coed, a settlement of slate houses and hotels with solid if unexciting Victorian comforts.    One feels that the place displays some effrontery to thus introduce itself into the heart of such superb glen and river scenery, though it sits quietly, almost respectfully, and is inoffensive enough.    Even in mid-summer there is little suggestion of hysterical tourism, though during recent years an enterprising local driver was organising trips by 'jeep' to Llyn Elsi. The track to the lake lies behind the Victorian Romanesque church, an ambitious structure by Paley and Austin, with some interesting details and a good setting, for the old church is no longer in normal use.    Below Pont-y-Pair, a fifteenth-century bridge over the Llugwy, which is here churned into white-flecked foam by a cauldron of rock, is the Royal Oak Hotel, wherein is preserved the signboard painted by David Cox. We have already had occasion to mention this painter, a lover of Welsh landscapes, who in his *Welsh Funeral* has caught the spirit of Wales more successfully than any other English painter.    The guest-books of Cox's time—from one of which some vandal has cut out Cox's original sketch for the signboard—are also preserved here and are of interest for the signatures of such people as Disraeli, Gladstone, Herkomer, Sir Henry Irving, Anthony Hope, President Roosevelt and others.    There are few interesting old houses in the immediate vicinity, but Ty'n y Cae, near the Fairy Glen, is a cottage which preserves such early features as a curious ingle built of wattle-work daubed with clay, a massive hooded fireplace with flanking slate slabs standing on end, an open timber roof and a door with original wooden pegs and latches.

Those who wish to see more of the Llugwy must take the Capel Curig road, and those who wish to follow the Conwy must cross Waterloo Bridge and push on to Pentre Voelas, at the foot of the wide grouse-moors, and the remote village of Yspytty Ifan, beyond which the Conwy rises from its lake on the edge of the Migneint moorlands.    But the valley of the Afon Machno too is worth exploring, pushing on beyond the much-lauded pandy-mill and falls to Penmachno, a grey-slate village tumbling about these wild moorlands.    Here there were once two churches in the same churchyard, but only a single modern church remains.    The Carausius stone is the most important of the early inscribed stones here, for Carausius, a humble Menapian, was a skilful seaman and commander, and one tradition has it that he was the real founder of the British Navy, *c.* 288.    Best of all, we would follow the Lledr, perhaps the

loveliest, certainly the most highly coloured, of all these rivers.   About
Bettws-y-Coed the valley is green and richly wooded, but beyond
Pont-y-pant it becomes wilder and the river rages over mountain-frag-
ments blocking its course.   There are birch-trees everywhere, and much
the same flowers and plants as we have seen beside the Llugwy, and there
is lush lowland vegetation in russet, mauve and purple clusters.   In the
quarrying village of Dolwyddelan, where Llewelyn the Great may have
been born, is the unrestored church erected by a Prince of Powys, its
interesting interior having a ribbed wood barrel-vault over the chancel,
a rood-screen with fifteenth-century traceried heads, the loft missing and
usurped by a Georgian balustrade, early-eighteenth-century furniture,
and a good screen-like Jacobean mural tablet, panelled and rouged and
gilded.   And beyond the village the Lledr flows beside the lonely square
embattled tower of Dolwyddelan, a native castle upon its crag.   Beyond again is the so-called Roman Bridge, and about it now are the
infinite moorlands.   The graceful peak of Moel Siabod appears northward.   Westward are hill-tracks to Beddgelert, and this charmed circle
is complete.

92   Anglesey Landscape, looking across the Menai Straits to the Mainland

93   South Stack Lighthouse (1809) on Holyhead Island

94 The Menai Straits, spanned by Thomas
Telford's Suspension Bridge (1826)

95 Church Island, Anglesey, with Robert Stephenson's
Tubular Bridge (1849) in the background

# XI

## EXCURSION INTO ANGLESEY

THE Menai Strait is so narrow that one is apt to forget that Anglesey is an island. Yet an island it is, and whether one reaches it by Telford's mighty suspension bridge (94) or by Stephenson's ringing tubular bridge (95), guarded by petrified lions, there is all the anticipation of a primitive sea-girt land. It was the last stronghold of the Druids and the last stronghold of the Welsh chieftains during the Edwardian Conquest, and it may well be the last stronghold of Welsh nationalism. It has not the dramatic contrasts, the flourishes and heights, of the mainland, but it has a drama all its own, the drama of elementals and of people living in close touch with soil and sea. For Goronwy Owen, greatest of Anglesey poets, it was "green-meadowed Môn of every land the loveliest land".

Near the end of the Menai Bridge is the characteristic church of Llantysilio on its spit of land laved by the Strait, the opposite shore fringed with firs. Llanfair P.G., the village with the apocalyptic (and apocryphal) name celebrated on comic postcards, is nearby, and the vicinity is dominated by the lofty monument, by Harrison of Chester, to the first Marquess of Anglesey, who commanded the cavalry at Waterloo and left a leg there. Plas Newydd, the old seat of the marquesses, was Gothicised by James Wyatt, and the front elevation has traceried windows, central turrets and side towers. Other interesting houses about here are Plas Coch, with sixteenth-century stepped gables, and Llanidan, and in the disused church of Llanidan is an ancient stone reliquary displaying the bones of an unknown saint. The village of Bryn Siencyn has an early nineteenth-century nucleus, of which all the cottages have uniform fan-lights, but the joy of this place is in its views of the massed mountains upon the mainland. We have chosen to negotiate a tangled network of country lanes, decked with honeysuckle and dog-rose, rather than follow the often monotonous main roads of the island. This area is rich in the prehistoric remains described so fully in Rowland's *Mona Antiqua*, and we begin to discover a Dutch abundance of derelict windmills. On the edge of Newborough Warren lies the somnolent village of Newborough, once a place of some importance, where until recently the villagers made ropes and nets from the sea-reed grass of the warren. Its church is largely

Decorated work, though like many Anglesey churches it contains an early font, and is notable for the effigy of a priest in eucharistic vestments. Southward stretch the sand dunes, with an occasional croft on the edge of a patch of salt marsh. The drowned wilderness stretches from the Cefn estuary to the breakwater at Aber Menai Point, and from the south of it runs the little peninsula known as Llanddwyn Island, for an island it virtually is. Here are the slight remains of a *clas*, a lighthouse and a colony of screeching sea-birds. Beyond the Cefn estuary, where the gardens and woods of Bodorgan slope down to the water, is Llangadwa-ladr, its medieval church having matured late Gothic additions and good stained glass in which local squires mingle with the Virgin Mary, St. David and St. John. On the tiny Ffraw river is Aberffraw, formerly a seat of Welsh princes, from which one may reach St. Cwfan's church, set on a rock-ribbed strand and islanded at high tide. And this is a solitary rock-walled church of elemental simplicity, catching at the heart and the imagination as more elaborate churches cannot do.

Holyhead Island is approached either by the Bangor road causeway or by the crossing from the Pen-y-bont inn. The latter reaches Holyhead by way of Trearddur Bay, which has become a playground for the sophis-ticated and the affluent, but which has natural charm enough, and its Stanley windmill of *c.* 1828 is yet working. Holyhead itself is a little bleary-eyed and lacking in character, though it has relics of earlier settlements, prehistoric, Roman and medieval. Its church of St. Cybi is of good Perpendicular work, with highly enriched porch and embattle-ments and a seventeenth-century tower, containing the effigy of a Stanley by Thornycroft. (One of the Stanleys became a Mohammedan, and it is said that several Anglesey churches contain Mohammedan glass from the East, though I have not yet found it.) Much of the massive granite churchyard wall is certainly Roman work (97), and it is a little odd, standing here, to look immediately down on to the harbour crowded with Irish mail-boats and hemmed in by dock buildings. The harbour is the work of Rennie, and at the entrance to the earlier pier is the triumphal marble arch of 1821 commemorating the landing of George IV. The north of the island is dominated by the sea-washed granite Holyhead Mountain with its purple-heathered crest, dotted eczema-like with *oytiau* or hut circles. (At Din Lligwy in north-east Anglesey is an excellent example of such an early settlement, enclosed by a pentagonal stone wall.) Fuchsia and hydrangeas blossom here, and occasionally rare plants grab a precarious foothold in the magnificent naked rocks of this coast. The formidable South Stack is crowned with the dazzling white-walled colony of the lighthouse-keepers (93), who have for company clouds of shriek-ing cormorants, guillemots and gulls.

The north-west of Anglesey is watered by the Alaw, rising in the snipe-bog of Cors y Bol, and beyond Bodedwern is Llyn Llywenan, perhaps the largest of the island's dozen or more lakes. Many of the

96 Penmon Priory, Anglesey (*left*)

97 The " Roman Arches " at the entrance
to the Parish Church, Holyhead (*below*)

98    Victoria Terrace, *c.* 1835.  *Joseph Hansom, architect*

99    The concentric Castle of Edward I

BEAUMARIS, ANGLESEY

villages round about, Llanfachraeth, Llanddeusant, Llanfaethlin, Llan-
fflewyn and others, are primitive hamlets, often whitewashed, each with
the characteristic church indicated in the village name. In Llanabo church
is the incised figure of its patron saint, St. Pabo, and at Llanfachell, where
serpentine marble is quarried, the church has Norman and later work,
and its tower has a beehive cap added by a Georgian squire who wished
to muffle an offending bell. The entire coast is indented with picturesque
coves and bays, and at Cemmaes Bay some old houses are clustered about
the quay, the tiny harbour and boat-yard largely protected by natural
spurs of rock; its church of Llanbadrig—or Patrick—crowns a distant
precipitous cliff. There is a maritime strip of good fertile land running
across the north of Anglesey, broken only by pigmy ranges of rock and
dotted with windmills, whitewashed farms, grey barns and gilded gorse.
It is in such country that we find, on the edge of Amlwch, a startling
functional church after Gropius or Le Corbusier, out of harmony with
its surroundings but original enough to be exciting. Amlwch itself is a
small town of fairly modern development, and its church, inns and
houses are of the late eighteenth century. The Dinorben Arms has a
plain but solid staircase of the period, and its porch is engraved with the
Greek fret or key-pattern so common in Anglesey. The church is a
hybrid combining Gothic and Classical. All this owes its inception to a
company which mined the Parys Mountain for copper, a local industry
which was prolific but short-lived. During the last century three tobacco
factories were also at work here. Amlwch today is a quiet market-town,
and its harbour is derelict, the houses and offices in ruins. This dead
port is a strange, awesome place, truly ghostly and affecting, particularly
so if one has seen old prints of its halcyon days.

On the way to Llaneilian are startling brilliantly coloured ships' figure-
heads, and the land is ribbed with rock and gilded with gorse. Cottages
and farms are whitewashed, and purplish veronica bursts from the hedges.
Beneath a spray of fuchsia pranking a farmhouse wall I found a coy peri-
winkle with silver-green leaves and a flower of even more vivid hue than
the veronica. In such country is the hamlet of Llaneilian, its church,
lych-gate, cross and walls, enclosing a rocky graveyard, all of silver-grey
stone, the ensemble strikingly Breton in character. The delightful
interior is rich in curios, containing a fifteenth-century rood-screen with
a dancing skeleton painted upon the loft, coeval benches and book-desks,
a black oak altar-table of 1634, corbelled figure-heads of bagpipers in the
chancel, and wrought-iron chandeliers and lamp-brackets. Adjoining
the church, connected by a slype or passage, is the chapel of St. Eilian,
recalling the chapel of St. Beuno at Clynnog in the Lleyn. Southward
rises the Parys Mountain above its chain of miniature lakes, and from
Nebo the distant mountains of Caernarvonshire seem filled with magic.
At the foot of Nebo Hill is Llanwenllwyfo, its church having an imposing
array of seventeenth-century stained-glass windows, and negotiating the

landlocked Traeth Dulas one comes to the Lilliputian harbour of Moelfre, with a handful of prudish cottages fringing a small arc of shingled beach. Llanallgo rectory received Dickens, whose *Uncommercial Traveller* relates the story of the clipper *Royal Charter* which was wrecked off Moelfre, and the curious church, over restored, has a thirteenth-century bell. Llanfair-mathafarn-eithaf, beyond the woodlands of Parcian, was the birthplace of Goronwy Owen, the tinker's son who went up to Jesus College, Oxford, was for ten years a curate in England, emigrated to Virginia in 1757 to become master of a Williamsburg college (a post he lost through drink), and rescued from oblivion the ancient forms of Welsh poetry.

From Llanfair the centre of the island may be explored, proceeding southward from Llanerchymedd, once noted for snuff and cattle-fairs, to Llangefni, a busy little market-town with a solid Victorian atmosphere. About Llangefni lies a group of villages with interesting churches— Llangristiolus, Cerrigceinwen, Llanbeulan and others; Llanbeulan church is archaic and tenebrous, with open timber roof and crude old benches. Midway between Llangefni and Pentraeth is Plas Penmynydd, the birth-place of Owen Tudor, the dancing law-student who captivated the heart of Catherine of Valois, widow of Henry V, and founded a family which for three generations sat upon the English throne. In the church are the effigies of Vychan, an ancestor of Owen, in armour and tilting helm, and his wife, who lies in the costume and three-cornered head-dress of the fifteenth century. Pentraeth and Red Wharf Bay, with its gleaming villas, now lie north-eastward. Near Pentraeth, where the Borrovian White Horse is no longer an inn, is Plas Gwyn, one of the most successful Georgian brick mansions in Wales and the only one of its kind in Anglesey, with excellent internal detail. Between here and Beaumaris are some grand vistas of Snowdonia, and these are enhanced at Beaumaris itself by the grape-coloured water of the Strait, especially when lashed to storm fury.

Beaumaris is a constant delight, and one cannot but praise it for con-triving to create the amenities of a seaside resort whilst judiciously pre-serving its historical *comble*. One's first impression is that it is a Regency watering-place, perhaps an early miniature of Brighton, for many of its houses are of that period, and the idiom lingers in the Victoria Terrace of 1836 by Joseph Hansom (98), the versatile architect who designed the Birmingham Town Hall (itself of Anglesey marble), the church of St. Phillip Neri at Arundel in Sussex, and the hansom cab. The Bulkeley Arms Hotel, with its pedimented windows, Greek porch and balcony (from which at the Anglesey Hunt meet hot coppers are thrown to the crowds below) is also by Hansom, and one suspects his hand in several houses. The Town Hall of 1808 and the gaol of 1829 are also eminently Classical, and in the latter the old treadmill is still *in situ*. This was the age of brocaded waistcoats and smoking-caps, many of which were worn in Beaumaris, but the town has a long history, and the earlier magpie architecture also colours its high street.    Court Mawr has a (later) wooden gallery corbelled out in Tyrolese fashion, an antique-shop has a coved gable, and both the Bull's Head and Liverpool Arms, though refronted, have seventeenth-century staircases, though of staircases one may prefer the essay in Georgian *chinoiserie* in Bishopsgate House.  The most intriguing of these buildings is the Court House of 1614, with its original stone paving, woodwork, balcony and coved ceiling and its Georgian Gothic windows.  Above and beyond them all is the castle (99), the last and most ingenious of the Edwardian fortresses—and the most perfect; still surrounded by its sea-water moat, its inner wall-passage recalling Caernarvon, and its vaulted apsidal oratory recalling that of Conway.

We have left ourselves little time in which to see the parish church, with its attractive stained glass and its monuments, Baron Hill, the Classical mansion attributed to James Wyatt, and the almshouses of Llanfaes.  For we must hasten to Penmon, where in the sixth century St. Seiriol founded the *clas* which later became an Augustinian monastery. The early Norman church, with pyramidal tower, is intact (96), and among the sculptures are symbols which someone has suggested are curiously akin to the salamander emblem of Francis I as seen at the Château de Blois.  The conventual buildings include fragments of the south and east claustral ranges, partly embodied in a farmhouse.  Nearby is a fine square dovecote of *c.* 1600 with domed vault and cupola, and northward is St. Seiriol's Well with a structure representing the saint's chapel.  In the deer park is an elaborate cross of *c.* 1100 with the key-pattern which so many Anglesey buildings have borrowed and with a sculptured Temptation of St. Anthony (a theme on which Flaubert wrote a classic variation).  At Penmon, the Malory of Sheridan Le Fanu's novel *Tenants of Malory*, we have left this mundane twentieth century, and if we would project ourselves yet further we have but to cross to Priestholme, 'Puffin Island', veritably the home of the *Alca arctica* of Linnaeus, with its blue hyacinths and its sea-fowl squatting on the sharp rock terraces, its round tower and its ruins of a hermit's oratory of early Irish inspiration.

# XII

## THE VALE OF CLWYD    DENBIGH AND ITS PURLIEUS    THE VALE OF LLANGOLLEN TOWNS AND VILLAGES OF FLINT

FROM Pentre Voelas on the road between Bettws-y-Coed and Corwen one may penetrate a northern moorland watered by a quartet of pellucid streams, the Alwen, Cledwen, Aled and Elwy. The terrain is often marshy and hung with low-flying mists, and Llyn Aled is rather elusive.    To north and east are reservoirs created from the Aled and the Alwen.    The Sportsman Inn is an oasis in this wilderness. Nantglyn, with its lovely yews, lies off the road to Llansannan.    Here were born David Samwell, surgeon to Captain Cook on the world-circling *Discovery*, and Mrs. Jordans, the eighteenth-century actress. These remote parishes are remarkable for their celebrities, and at Llansannan were born no less than four distinguished Welshmen—Tudor Aled, William Salusbury, William Rees and Henry Rees.    The village has a tiny square and the black and white stone Plas yn Cornel, formerly the dower house of Dyffryn Aled.    Across the hills, where the Aled festoons a dingle with pretty cascades, is charming Llanfair Talhaiarn, facing the wooded park of Garthewin, where the old barn now witnesses to masses and Welsh mystery-plays and where the *Nosen Lawen*, or traditional social evenings, have been revived by Robert Wynne.    About here are the billowing Hiraethog Hills, covered with crimson heather in mid-summer, and in the valley of the Elwy the lanes are fringed with hazels.

Before entering the Vale of Clwyd we should contrive to see a group of country houses in this area.    They are all pastiches, all later than the eighteenth century.    Gwrych Castle, a gleaming white fantasy of limestone set amid cypresses and larch, was completed in the year of Waterloo. Intended to be a replica of an Edwardian fortress, it has the appearance of a giant folly, and many of its eighteen towers are merely shells.    The whole is embattled and turreted and lighted by traceried windows of Perpendicular design, and the curtain walls, though unconvincing, are highly picturesque.    The internal decoration is of the Regency, and there is an excellent marble grand staircase, reputedly Italian work, with dadoes

100  In the Vale of Llangollen, Denbighshire

101 Rhuddlan Castle, Flintshire

102 Chirk Castle, in the Denbighshire landscape

surmounted by filigreed iron-work. Kinmel Hall, with its ornamental iron palisades, was designed by Thomas Hopper; and Bodelwyddan Hall, castellated and many-turreted, is another of the clan. The Victorian Gothic church of Bodelwyddan by John Gibson, a pupil of Barry, far eclipses in popular esteem anything in the vicinity. It is a graceful building in English Decorated, though there is some Flemish influence, and the diversity of rich colourful mediums makes of it a thing of vigorous and lyrical beauty. Itself of limestone, this church is graced with the creamy Talacre stone, the darker Caen stone and alabaster, Purbeck black marble, Belgian red marble and the brilliant Carrara and Languedoc marbles. It is perhaps exotic and sensational, but much to be preferred to most Victorian work.

Rhuddlan lies at the head of the Vale of Clwyd, but one should make a detour to Dyserth, straggling at the foot of limestone bastions. Here there are slight remains of a castle crowning a scarped height rich in rare plants, and below are the ruins of Siamber Wen, an old stone house which reflects the arrangements of late Norman manorial houses. The medieval church is enriched by a Jesse window, and in the churchyard are some fine specimens of tomb-craft, some barrel-vaulted and others like Jacobean tables on carved balusters. The stream, footbridge and cascades make an attractive picture, and there are a few thatched and white-washed weavers' cottages. Until last century Rhuddlan was a busy port, but today it is deserted, a little crestfallen, a little decrepit. Yet its name is immortal, for it is linked with the melancholy Welsh air *Morfa Rhuddlan*, a folk-song which bewails the massacre of the Welsh by Offa's Saxons on these alluvial flats. The castle is an Edwardian fortress of strictly concentric type (101), though lacking in the interest of its contemporaries. The church is largely thirteenth-century work and is of the parallel-nave type common in the vale. There are slight remains of a Dominican friary, a medieval dwelling reputedly a 'parliament house', and a few old houses such as the 'Gwindy' or wine-house.

We have entered the Vale of Clwyd, one of the most placid of Welsh valleys, often idyllic, with far-flung pasture lands dotted with white-washed farms and cottages, its eastern perimeter well defined by the long ridges of the Clwydian Mountains. St. Asaph lies on a hill between the Clwyd and the Elwy, and, like St. David's, is remarkable for being a village with a cathedral. This tiny cathedral is of ancient foundation, and the Victorian diocesan appendages, palace, deanery, canonry, etc., all of grey stone, gabled and mullioned, do their utmost to give the little place the air of a cathedral city. The effect is quite convincing, and St. Asaph has thus a unique character. The cathedral occupies the site of an early *clas*, the church of which was one of the very few places in Britain in which the *Laus Perennis*, the perpetual choral recital of the Divine Office by night and day, was maintained. The cathedral de-scribed by Giraldus was destroyed a century later, and the existing fabric is the rebuilt church of the late thirteenth century, with some Georgian interference and the inevitable patchwork by Scott. Certainly it it more satisfying than that of Bangor, for it has a good clerestory, excellent window tracery, creditable fittings and a pleasant trim exterior, a kind of Eleanor Cross rising from its lawn. The parish church is apt to be overlooked, though it is attractive, with twin naves and an excellent hammer-beam roof, while across the seventeenth-century bridge is the Old Deanery, with its 'Gothick' vaults. At nearby Llannerch the seventeenth-century terraced and turreted gardens have gone, and the Elizabethan house was altered by a Georgian squire with an itch for Romanticism and the Italianate. Cefn Hall is entirely Georgian, and the delights of this place are the limestone caverns with their fossils and their grand vistas of the distant Elwy valley.

The purlieus of St. Asaph are of much interest. From Tremeirchion, perched on the slopes of the Clwydian range, the vale is spread out away and below, a study in green and white, and a joy when dappled by sunlight, the whitewashed farms glinting and agleam. The church here is delightful, simple, single-naved and bell-coted, with a delicious vista through the lych-gate along the avenue of clipped yews to the timbered porch. It has the unique dedication, in England and Wales, of Corpus Christi, and its walls have a curious inverted 'batter', sloping downward and inward (or so it seems to me, but perhaps this is an illusion). The fourteenth-century effigy of Dafydd Ddu Hiraddug, cleric, poet and savant, is canopied, and the face of the tomb is carved with escutcheons displaying the Instruments of the Passion. Both Gabriel Piozzi and his wife, the former Mrs. Thrale, lie here. The remains of Bachegraig, a pyramidal house formerly held by the Salusburys, are nearby, as is Brynbella, the Georgian villa where lived Mrs. Thrale (herself a Salusbury). Beyond Tremeirchion crags of limestone rise from the tilted fields, and on the utmost height is St. Beuno's chapel, an effective bit of pastiche in Tyrolean manner. Celandines nod in the lanes, and there is the song of the chaffinch and the blue-tit in the woods about St. Beuno's College. This is a Jesuit seminary designed by Joseph Hansom, of local stone, dormered, mullioned and buttressed. The grounds are carpeted with daffodils, and these flowers are massed upon the chapel altar. The beautiful cross of St. Beuno, early-fifteenth-century work, with fine tabernacled head, was originally in the churchyard of Tremeirchion. The seminary has acquired some lustre on account of its associations with Gerard Manley Hopkins, the poet. A Jesuit priest, Hopkins took his three years' theology here, preferring Duns Scotus to Aristotle in the library, and often writing in Welsh metres. He was a poet's poet, a theoretician whose verse may perhaps have owed not a little to his friend Bridges.

The white roads of this limestone country lead to many a charming village, to Caerwys, perhaps the Roman Varoe, to Nannerch, with its

103   The splendid fifteenth-century Parish Church of Wrexham, Denbighshire

104   A Half-timbered Farmhouse, Plas-yrn-Pentre, Denbighshire

105, 106    Kneeling Figures on the Monument to Sir Richard Trevor (1638)
at Gresford Church, Denbighshire

107    The Tomb of Sir John Salusbury (1578) at Whitchurch, Denbighshire

church spire embowered in chestnut-trees, to idyllic Bodfari at the foot
of Moel Gaer.   Here the River Wheeler cuts through a deep gorge and
there is a configuration of glen, stream and woodland, and there are
yellow iris flowers and the song of thrushes.   Beyond Trefnant, with its
toy industry, is Denbigh, high on the western edge of the vale.   This
attractive county town has a high street of singular character, for one
side of it is jettied over Georgian colonnades, no doubt inspired by the
earlier Rows of Chester, and Denbigh citizens have a delightful habit
of referring to it as 'the piazza'.   Though Georgian brick and Palladian
windows predominate, much of the fabric is Elizabethan or earlier.
The Bull Hotel has a remarkable Elizabethan staircase, with gloved hands
carved on the newel posts; the Golden Lion inn has fifteenth-century
timber-framing; and the Back Row Hotel has a plaster overmantel of
1643 carved with the double-headed eagle.   The severe late-Georgian
Town Hall embodies part of its sixteenth-century predecessor.   Perhaps
the most novel structure here is the Georgian cock-pit behind the Hawk
and Buckle Inn.   This is circular, of stone with conical roof thatched
with straw.   It is less elegant than that at Conway, but is in perfect
preservation.   Though cock-fighting had been revived at the Restoration,
it did not become common until the late eighteenth century, and the
Welsh method of staging a cock-fight, known as the 'Welsh main', was
particularly brutal.   Relics of cock-fighting, together with the Rules,
may be seen in the Castle Hotel at Ruthin.

But Denbigh, like Janus, is two-faced, for on the western side of the
town is the medieval walled borough with its castle.   The castle is of
the thirteenth and fourteenth centuries, with a fine triangular gatehouse
having three polygonal towers, the ball-flower ornament around the
seated figure of (?) Edward I above the arch also being unusual.   The
town walls are coeval but are now incomplete, the Burgesses' Tower,
with some remarkable buttressing, being the sole remaining gateway.
Nearby are the solitary tower of the garrison chapel of St. Hilary, of
c. 1300, and the ruins of an unfinished church founded by the Earl of
Leicester, to whom Elizabeth gave the lordship of Denbigh.   The castle
and walls, dominated by the splendid Goblin Tower, are best seen from
the foot of the rocky bluff and from the purlieus of Howell's School,
belatedly built in 1850 from a fund of Spanish ducats left in trust by a
local draper who died in Seville in 1540.   The handsome main building
has a green-and-mauve striped roof and the schoolgirls wear multi-
coloured uniforms.

The mother-church of St. Marcellus stands away from the town; it is
of fifteenth- and sixteenth-century date, twin-naved, with an excellent
hammer-beam roof, carvings of sheep-shearing, and a fresco depicting
plainsong notation.   There is a mural tablet to Thomas Edwards (Twm
o'r Nant), who became turnpike-keeper and bricklayer, was early
influenced by Bunyan, and wrote some celebrated interludes, those folk-

plays of the late eighteenth century.  Another monument portrays
Humphrey Lloyd, the scholarly antiquarian who issued the first printed
map of England and Wales (he was a friend of Ortelius, the Dutch
publisher, who in 1570 produced the first printed world atlas).

The country around Denbigh is rich in old houses.  Among them are
Plas Chambers, with fifteenth-century panelling and Queen Anne
plaster arabesques; Plas Clough, the home of Sir Richard Clough,
adventurer, astronomer and co-founder with Sir Thomas Gresham of
the Royal Exchange; the Jacobean Old Foxhall, home of Humphrey
Lloyd; New Foxhall, a folly of 1608 now given over to rooks and
daffodils; and Galch Hill, the birthplace of Sir Hugh Myddleton, who
brought the New River to London, and of his brother, Sir Thomas,
Lord Mayor of London.  Lawnt is a delectable hamlet of whitewashed
cottages hidden among woodlands, beside a rippling stream with hyacinths
on its banks.  Above the glades of gorse and laurel is Gwaenynog, an old
mansion of the Myddletons, where schoolgirls take lessons in a Georgian
*salon* with a delicately patterned floral ceiling, while at least one bedroom
has a coved ceiling of similar design.  Dr. Johnson was here, and in a
nearby glade is an inscribed Grecian urn to his memory, erected by his
host before the sage had a chance to die, a gesture which occasioned some
caustic remarks from the startled doctor.

At Llanrhaiadr is a homely group comprising corbie-stepped hall,
whitewashed cottages elbowing the old King's Arms, fine old lych-gate
and church, the latter of local type with a brilliantly coloured Jesse
window.  The long Clwydian range ripples eastward on the way to
Ruthin, a warmly coloured town of red and grey stone.  Here the streets
converge upon a market-square rich in domestic architecture.  The
restored timber-framed Council House of 1401 is now a bank, but the
early-eighteenth-century White Lion yet functions as the Castle Hotel,
its lofty brick façade laced with stone.  Adjoining it is the former
Myddleton Arms, timber-framed, with a Georgian penthouse, its singular
high-pitched tiled roof having three rows of dormers at varying elevations.
Looking from a side window of the hotel across this dormered red roof,
with the broached church spire in the background, one falls under the
illusion that this is Flanders.  And quite justifiably, since the Myddleton
Arms was built by that Sir Richard Clough alluded to above, who built
a number of houses in this area directly based upon Flemish models.
Beyond are the scrolled and gilded gates, by the Davies brothers, fronting
the churchyard.  The church is twin-naved and contains an enriched
lacunar roof *temp.* Henry VII and a bust of Gabriel Goodman, a native
who became Dean of Westminster under Elizabeth.  Goodman founded
the rebuilt almshouses and the old Grammar School, now disused but
retaining panelling and desks of *c.* 1700.  The so-called Cloisters adjoining
the church embody portions of a medieval ecclesiastical college forming
the residence of the Warden or incumbent.  Jetted porch-wings are

singularly prominent in Ruthin, and Castle Street is particularly rich in Georgian and earlier houses. Nantclwyd House is an attractive specimen of late-sixteenth-century timber-framing, its porch-wing jettied over later Ionic pillars and its panelled hall having a gallery. The Wynnstay Arms is a Borrovian inn with some attractive late-sixteenth-century woodwork. The County Gaol of 1755 by Turner of Chester (whose 'House of Correction' at Hawarden is admirable) is worth looking at, as is the County Hall of 1785, a neat civic essay in Roman Doric with little triumphal arches at the sides. For the rest there are the castle ruins, a late-thirteenth-century irregular pentagon with five drums on the curtain, in the grounds of a chocolate-coloured mansion of last century. I find Ruthin a pleasant place to be in, as presumably did the caretaker who said to Mrs. Thrale when she intimated that she was going to Ruthin: "Ruthin, mum, my wife came from Ruthin, and when she died I made up my mind I'd go with the body to Ruthin, for I thought I would find it a pleasant journey, and indeed, mum, I found it a very pleasant journey."

Across the Clwyd rise the broad purple ridge of Moel Llech, the cone of Moel Gyw, the steep heathery Moel Fenlli, and their queen, Moel Fammau, with its little copse of trees and the storm-shattered monument by Harrison of Chester commemorating George III's jubilee. About their foothills lie many village Arcadies, where until recent years local customs and traditions were tenaciously maintained. Throughout the vale there were Morris dancers fantastically attired in coloured ribbons, who on May-day danced through the village to the tune of a tin whistle. In Llangynhaval church the elders of the parish households sat on chairs before the communion table, while the others were allocated, according to seniority and social rank, to the rear pews. There are jonquil-coloured cottages about Llanbedr, and at Llanrhydd, where the white, rambling hall was the home of Stanley Weyman, the novelist, the church has a monument with a hierarchy of fourteen children dutifully kneeling in memory of their departed parents. At Llanfair, embowered in pine-trees, the church is of Clwydian type and contains a good roof and a mosaic window of old glass. Nearby are the lovely incomplete Elizabethan house of Llwyn Ynn and the Jesus Chapel, built in the puritan idiom of the late eighteenth century and having a Classical entrance in which Gothic detail lingers. About Eyarth the Clwyd becomes a mountain stream cutting through a limestone gorge, and from the terraced Eyarth Rocks the vale is seen spread-eagled northward.

Corwen sits lazily below the last outcrop of the Berwyns, unexciting save for its cattle fairs and its prize sheep-dog trials. Its black-and-white striped stone inns are of the eighteenth century, and its church has been severely mishandled by the restorers. Yet at Rhug nearby is one of the most colourful and ornate manorial chapels in the Kingdom. Of 1637, it is rich in woodwork, with curious and crude devices painted in brilliant colours, the work of local craftsmen. It contains an open timber roof with angel purlins, a balustraded altar-rail flanked by elaborate boxed-in squirearchal pews, a pulpit fixed in a screen, the whole panelled and painted, with Welsh inscriptions and grisly *memento mori*, original seating with raised sides carved with scriptural animals, and a (later) fine spiked candelabrum of wood, probably by the same craftsman who made that at Pennant Melangell. Bala lies along the Dee valley, beyond Cynwyd, where young ramblers sleep in the loft of the old flannel-mill and perform chilly dawn ablutions in the mill-race. This is fine tramping country, and my last memory of it is of John Cowper Powys, the modern Merlin of these hills, who wanders early each morning over the Berwyns and who, when I last saw him, was writing a monumental historical novel centred about Corwen.

North-eastward the Dee flows below the Llantysilio Mountain and describes a celebrated bend near Llantysilio village. We have reached the Vale of Llangollen (100), which has been so lauded by topographers that it were a pity to here waste valuable time and space. Llangollen itself is an indifferent town blessed with a girdle of steep hills and the passage of the friendly Dee, while for many of us the china plates and jugs embossed with the steeple-hatted figures of the Ladies of Llangollen have become part of the salvage of our childhood. Lady Eleanor Butler and the Hon. Sarah Ponsonby, "certainly the most celebrated virgins in Europe", as Prince Puckler-Muskau described them, were Irish gentlewomen who appeared in Llangollen about 1776 and lived there for over half a century. They wore their hair powdered, short and uncurled, wearing male hats and cravats, boots and blue riding-habits. They had a genuine and quite romantic affection for each other and were charming blue-stockings, but there appears to be some evidence that their way of life was artfully designed to bring mercenary advantages. Plas Newydd, their *cottage orné*, was the scene of social gatherings resembling the *salons* of Mesdames de Sévigné and de Maintenon, but its pretty façade and faked timbering no longer screen such brilliance and intrigue. Llangollen and Corwen were noted for harp music, no longer heard except at infrequent soirées where a privileged few hear it in a form revived by Arnold Dolmetsch. Both Borrow and Kilvert heard a harpist living in Llangollen who played several times daily in the Hand Hotel, and Kilvert stated (1871) that this was the only hotel in Wales with a Welsh harpist. For the treble-stringed Welsh harp was already going out of use, giving way to the easier double-stringed English harp. It was at the Hand Hotel that Hazlitt sat down to read Rousseau's *La Nouvelle Héloise* over a bottle of sherry and a cold chicken. The Dee flows under a fourteenth-century bridge and passes below the shale fragments of Castell Dinas Bran, rich in legend and possibly pre-Celtic, heading now for the marshy flats of its estuary.

We would do better to take the road across the Llandegla moorlands, which provides a good pretext for seeing Eliseg's Pillar, the most celebrated inscribed stone in Wales, and the ruins of Valle Crucis, its charming setting comparable with Tintern. Founded about 1200, its ground plan, design and ornament are strikingly similar to those of its English Cistercian contemporaries. The church is fairly complete, the west front having a nice composition of plate-tracery windows and rose window. The eastern claustral range remains, comprising sacristy, a perfect vaulted chapter-house and slype, with a well-preserved upper storey containing the dorter. At Llandegla, where a black cock was frequently sacrificed to St. Tegla, is the old Crown Inn, a holy well and a village green, and at Llanarmon the church contains the effigy of an abbot of Valle Crucis and a medieval bronze chandelier with a small statue of the Virgin. Mold may be reached via the Loggerheads Inn with its signboard painted by Richard Wilson, who lies in Mold churchyard. The county town of Flintshire has a picturesque tree-planted high street and a fifteenth-century church, with a Georgian tower, containing good glass and roof and friezes carved with animals. Daniel Owen, whose novels portray the authentic Welsh life of last century, was a native. In the vicinity are many good houses, among them the fifteenth-century embattled Tower with a Queen Anne addition, Rhual, of 1634, its formal garden having crested spikes of iron, some flower-shaped, on the garden walls, and Gwysaney and Leeswood, both with gates by the Davies family (78). The Leete, the lovely valley of the upper Alyn, which here separates the ore-seamed Halkin Mountain from the Clwydian range, may be followed to Cilcain. Beyond Northop—and one must not forget that George Eliot's father was a Northop man—is Flint, an industrial town on the muddy banks of the Dee estuary. Its castle, built with the town as a *bastide*, is lapped by tidal water and is unique in plan, its great circular donjon having affinities with the Tour de Constance at Aigues Mortes in Provence. It provides the setting of the capture of Richard II in Shakespeare's play, and there is an entertaining account of the fugitive king's meeting with Bolingbroke here in *A History of the Deposition of Richard II*, in French verse, in the Harleian MSS.

Near Holywell are the scanty remains of yet another Cistercian monastery, Basingwerk Abbey, with little but its thirteenth-century arcaded refectory. There is more to detain us in Holywell, a miniature Lourdes and a study for the teratologist. For here is the well of St. Winefride, a copious spring traditionally reputed to have welled up on the site of St. Winefride's averted martyrdom, her severed head, lopped off by the seducing Caradoc, miraculously restored by St. Beuno. The exquisite chapel is attributed to the piety of Lady Margaret Beaufort, mother of Henry VII, and is in that matured Gothic which in Wales reached its apogee both here and at Mold (in both places the animal friezes are strikingly akin). The medieval bath is in the crypt, but the pilgrims use the large wooden bath before the chapel, and votive offerings decorate the walls. In Well Street the Georgian houses have doors made up of moulded octagonal panels, and in one of these houses, the former vicarage, lived Mary Land, daughter of a Vicar of Holywell. She left Flintshire for the chilly splendours of White Russia, and in 1801 was married to Andrew Voronȳkhin, one of the chief court architects of St. Petersburg. Nor have we yet done with the Roman, for at Pantasaph is a Franciscan friary partly designed by Augustus Welby Pugin, the white gabled buildings set between the grey hills and the pine woods where larks sing. One recalls the terraces of Assissi and the Madonna del Sasso above Locarno. Francis Thompson, the poet, lived by the monastery gates, and often when the sun was setting over Moel Fammau and the Vale of Clwyd he would pace about the calvary and recite his *Ode to the Setting Sun*. The area is rich in holy wells, and among local features is the old watch-tower or pharos on the wooded hill of Garreg, and the Maen Achwynfan (Stone of Lamentation), a penitential wheel-cross of the tenth century. The ruins of Downing Hall, the home of Pennant, are nearby, while Benedictine nuns now make their orisons in the Mostyn mansion at Talacre.

Lower Flintshire is a domain of red brick, paper-mills, lime-kilns, zinc-works and lead-mines, but amid the dross are hidden treasures: medieval glass at Trydden and Gresford, an old Quaker chapel at Cefn, castles at Hawarden and Caergwrle, and, farther south, the mansions of Erddig and Emral. Erddig is of 1683, with Georgian additions and a remodelling of the façade by Wyatt. The house has curiously emblazoned walls and magnificent furniture and carved gilt mirrors by Gumley and Moore. There is little left of Emral (79) for it was recently demolished (part of it being transplanted to Portmeirion), and an intriguing house it was, with its charming little sentinel-boxes with cupola-shaped roofs, and its coved drawing-room ceiling enriched with the Labours of Hercules.

But we have crossed the Dee and are virtually in England. Wales now lies westward, its serried hills faintly gleaming.

# INDEX

(Numerals in heavy type refer to *figure numbers* of illustrations)